Faces of Oppression and the Price of Justice

Faces of Oppression and the Price of Justice

A Woman's Journey from Eritrea to Saudi-Arabia and the United States

Dawit Okubatsion Woldu
&
Irvin H. Bromall

THE RED SEA PRESS
Trenton | London | New Delhi | Cape Town | Nairobi | Addis Ababa | Asmara | Ibadan

THE RED SEA PRESS
541 West Ingham Avenue | Suite B
Trenton, New Jersey 08638

Book design: Lemlem Taddese
Cover design: Ashraful Haque

Library of Congress Cataloging-in-Publication Data

Names: Woldu, Dawit Okubatsion, 1976- author. | Bromall, Irvin H., 1941-2014, author.
Title: Faces of oppression and the price of justice : a woman's journey from Eritrea to Saudi-Arabia and the United States / Dawit Okubatsion Woldu & Irvin H. Bromall.
Description: Trenton : The Red Sea Press, 2017. | Includes bibliographical references and index.
Identifiers: LCCN 2016038057| ISBN 9781569025031 (hb : alk. paper) | ISBN 9781569025048 (pb : alk. paper)
Subjects: LCSH: Natsnet, 1975- | Women refugees--Eritrea. | Women refugees--United States. | Household employees--Abuse of--Saudi Arabia. | Human smuggling. | Eritreans--Saudi Arabia. | Eritreans--United States. | Eritrea--Emigration and immigration. | Eritrea--Politics and government.
Classification: LCC JV8996.5 .W65 2017 | DDC 362.87089289073--dc23
LC record available at https://lccn.loc.gov/2016038057

DEDICATION

Dawit dedicates this book to Irv Bromall, the co-author of this book, who passed away early 2014 while this book project was in progress and to all those brave Eritrean men and women who seek, have sought, and continue to seek freedom from tyranny, horrors, and hardships both in their country and outside of their borders. We hope that this book will help to make others aware of current day Eritrea's desperate situation and the state of female domestic workers in the Gulf countries, and help to empower people of good will everywhere to build a new Eritrea. We also hope our work will make others aware of the struggle and challenges asylum seekers and other immigrants constantly face to get their legal status in the US.

CONTENTS

PREFACE

It was initially planned that Natsnet would be included on this book as co-author. Natsnet expressed great enthusiasm that Dawit and Irv tell her story, but she also equally expressed great fear of retaliation by the Eritrean government against her family, still in Eritrea. Her fears were legitimate and respected by the authors. Both authors emphasize that without Natsnet's contributions and willing cooperation, this book could not have become a reality and they again express their great gratitude to her.

To protect Natsnet's family, her real identity has been carefully disguised in the telling of her story. All characters mentioned, except for Irv and Dawit, have been given pseudonyms. In addition, throughout our presentation of Natsnet's story we try to establish a general sense of a world picture. Sometimes those depictions are enhanced of the times she experienced, and not record a complete history. We base this on our in-depth interviews with Natsnet and other women with similar experience, our reconstruction of their life's story, on other interviews with homeland and diaspora Eritreans who directly experienced this period in Eritrea's history, and on asylum declarations of several Eritreans. Contributing greatly were Dawit's life experiences, which led to his flight from Eritrea in 2003.

ACKNOWLEDGEMENT

The authors, Dawit O. Woldu and Irvin H. Bromall, extend their gratitude and thanks to our editor at Africa World Press and The Red Sea press.

We would like to thank Dr. Steve Howard, Dr. Ghirmai Negash, Dr. Faye Harrison, Dr. Zelalem Haile, Dr. Christine Kovic, Dr. Maria Curtis, Dr. Christine Walther, Dr. Hunt Davis, and Dr. Shreerekha Subramanian for their intellectual motivation and wonderful discussion, and constructive comments during the initial and during the writing process of this book. Our special thanks go to Dr. Christal Seahorn who tremendously helped us on editing the manuscript and creating the camera-ready format. She is an editorial mastermind and she was extremely helpful to improve the quality of this book. We would like to thank Ms. Rebecca Ruiz for proofreading before the final submission of the manuscript. Dawit would like also to thank friends and family members who have provided their full support.

Irv extends thanks to all those who put up with him as this project progressed. Special thanks are due to Dr. Lou Pech, whose contributions enhanced this work greatly. Irv thanks Dave Eggeling and his parents Teresa and Cliff and his brother Jim for their unbound love and support during this process. Irv also thanks to friends and the community in Moab Utah who showed him so much love and care.

Even though we did not include the comic pictures, the authors would like to extend our thanks to Mr. Benjamin Dix and his organization positivenegatives.org, for his willingness to give us the permission to use one of their comic stories on an Ethiopian maid working in Saudi Arabia. The authors also greatly appreciate Mr. Dix for providing very insightful information about the experiences of women maid workers in Saudi Arabia.

Finally, we would like to thank to the unanimous reviewers who provided us very constructive and useful comments to improve the quality of our work.

CHAPTER 1. INTRODUCTION

Forced Migration[1] and human trafficking (trafficking in persons)[2] are problematic for both sending and receiving countries but the largest burden of these problem is experienced by individuals and communities already suffering from poverty, political repression, and gender based violence. Migrants and refugees not only encounter great suffering in fleeing violence and oppression, but life continues to be a challenge after they reach their destination, especially in the western world. These challenges range from establishing legal status to cultural and linguistic barriers, poverty, racism, as well as associated health issues. To that end our work's main objective is to examine the political and social pathways to immigration and human trafficking in the Middle East and sub-Saharan Africa. This work also addresses some of the socio-cultural, economic, legal, and health difficulties migrants encounter once they arrive in the United States and Europe. More importantly the main goal of this book is to highlight the economic and political forces that push women from developing countries to seek work in oil rich Middle Eastern countries. This book is centered in the story of one female migrant, Natsnet (pseudonym), who left Eritrea for Saudi Arabia as a domestic worker and eventually arrived in the United States. Natsnet comes from a middle class Eritrean family, and was forced to choose to go to Saudi Arabia as a domestic worker instead of joining the Eritrean army as a national service recruit. Through her story and that of other Eritrean refugees, the book examines not only the difficulties migrants face in their journey to freedom but also their relentless struggles to cope with life once they arrive in host countries.

Migration (especially smuggler assisted migration[3]) and human trafficking have caused massive suffering for many communities in the developing world. The International Organization on Migration reports that the number of international migrants worldwide increased by 50% between 1990 and 2013, which is equivalent to an increase of more than 77 million individuals (UN 2013). The same report shows that much of the spike in migration occurred between 2000 and 2010. Similarly, the United Nations Office on Drug and Crime (UNDOC 2014) reported during the same period that incidents of human trafficking significantly increased both in number and distribution. Although no clear figure exists on how many of these migrations are trafficked or smuggler assisted, it is known that many were trafficked or smuggler assisted, particularly in areas around the Mediterranean Sea, Red Sea, and the Pacific. According to the United Nations on Drug and Trafficking 2014 report, 75% of human trafficking migrants from Asia and Sub-Saharan Africa are unskilled laborers (mostly domestic workers), and the majority of them are destined for oil rich Gulf countries (UNDOC 2014:81-83). The issues of refugees and migrants' crises is even worse now as millions of refugees from Syria, Eritrea, and Afghanistan are flooding the shores of Europe. Thousands of people are dying in seas and deserts in the hands of human traffickers.

Syria and Eritrea are the leading countries affected by migration facilitated by human traffickers in the Mediterranean Sea (United Nations Commission on Human Rights Report June 2015). While Syria is suffering from recurrent political violence, Eritreans are fleeing a repressive government that requires endless national service from its youth and denies its populace basic freedoms. National service is a compulsory military service that was introduced in 1994 by the Eritrean government to enlist both males and females between the ages of 18 and 50. Initially, the national service was planned for 18 months but practically everyone, who was conscripted since its inception is kept indefinitely in a very harsh condition that many reports compare to slavery or forced labor (The Economist, 2014, Kibreab 2009, UN Commission of Inquiry Report on Human Rights in Eritrea, 2015). The current mass exodus of Eritreans is a manifestation of growing human rights violations that began with the country's independence. Fundamentally, the history of migration since the creation of an Eritrean state stems from political repression and the never ending national service the country introduced in mid-1990. UNHCR estimates there are hundreds of thousands of Eritrean migrants who left Eritrea in recent years, but mass migration in Eritrea started long before the recent waves of hostage based trafficking[4] both in Sinai (destined for Israel) and Libya (destined for Europe) (Reisen and Rijken 2015, Brhane 2015, Mekonnen and Estfanos 2011). Prior to establishing independence, many Eritreans fled their home country due to the long war of independence from Ethiopia. Eritreans migrated to Gulf States in the Middle East and sought refuge in Europe, the United States, and Australia. Thousands of Eritreans, mostly women, have migrated to Saudi Arabia and other Gulf countries since the mid 1990's. The migrants were attracted to Saudi Arabia by the need for domestic workers in contrast to the lack of economic opportunities at home. After the late 1990's, most Eritrean women migrated to Saudi Arabia and the Middle East to avoid the endless national service requirements and the deteriorating human rights conditions in Eritrea. Furthermore, the Eritrean government encouraged these migrations to collect taxes and other remittances from its citizens working as domestic workers in the Saudi Arabia and other Gulf countries. Most of these migrations are well coordinated by the Eritrean government and their Saudi Arabian counterparts. Natsnet, the main character of this book, was a domestic worker whose migration to Saudi Arabia was partly arranged by her own government and the Saudi Arabian *Kafela* system, which brings domestic workers from impoverished third world countries to Saudi Arabia. Natsnet is part of the Eritrean migration fabric, which is primarily perpetuated by the Eritrean government's desire not only to control its citizens but also to gain the maximum economic and political support from its people once they leave the country's borders.

Migration impacts overall social and political structures of a country. The impact can be seen on at least three levels: the family, community, and government. From an anthropological perspective, the impact of migration due to political and economic hardships could change family dynamics, as well as the social and economic relationship within communities. From a family perspective, migration not only depletes family resources but also results in the loss of a productive member of the family and the disruption of the social support system. Children grow up without a father or a mother, and these children could end up on the streets in the urban areas or working as child laborers in rural villages. The pain of growing up far from one or both parents means the loss of family bond and absence of close adult mentorship in their lives.

The issue of migration and human trafficking can be approached from different disciplinary perspectives. Historically, different disciplines have approached migration from their own specific theoretical perspectives (Brettell and Hollified 2014:2). To that end, this research attempts to understand the social, cultural, legal, institutional, and personal trauma implications of migration from critical anthropology and political science perspectives (Whitten 1988, Taussing, 1987, Afifi 2011, Farmer 2004, Singer 2008). Expansive research has been done regarding the reasons for migration, particularly toward the western world, with a large portion of the literature focusing on the economic variables such as the "push" and "pull" economic theory (Molho 2013, Jenkins 1977, Doerschler 2006, Margolis 1994). This theory argues that migration is influenced by economic conditions both in the host and home countries. However, our work attempts to add to the growing literature on the broader socio-political factors (political push-pull factors Doeschler 2006) in order to shed light on the complexity of migration from the developing world, especially from sub-Saharan Africa and the Middle East. A large part of migration from some parts of the developing world, particularly the Horn of Africa and parts of the Middle East (e.g. Syria, Iraq, Palestine, and Libya), is driven by refugees arriving in Europe through smuggler assisted migrations. This complex migration phenomenon can be broadly explained by local and global political dynamics, as well as historical injustices that forced people to seek a better life somewhere else. Despite the existence of an international convention and scientific definitional differences between economic migrants and refugees, all migrants face similar experiences while living in their host countries. Understanding how migration patterns affect migrants' social, cultural, health, and economic life in their host country is an important research agenda and should be understood in the context of critical migration theory. Therefore, our work is grounded in a critical theory in migration study focusing on the historical, political and social forces that played into the complex web of factors that led to Natsnet's journey from Eritrea to Saudi Arabia, and finally to the United States. Our work also explores this migration phenomenon from a cross-cultural communication theory (Kalin 1986, Kleinman 1981, Fadiman 1998) that focuses on how culture based miscommunication becomes a major factor in immigration legal matters and other social issues, such as health and social relationships.

Methodologically, our work is grounded on narrative ethnography (Hampshire et al. 2014) and participant observation (Johnson et al. 2006, Gunn and Logstrup 2014, Dewalt and Dewalt 2011). Our narrative ethnography focused on collecting longitudinal semi-structured and unstructured interviews (Bernard 2013:360-390) and using those interviews to construct Natsnet's life history and her life experience. These narrative ethnographic interviews focus on Natsnet's understanding of the different social and political realities she experienced in her home country and her journey as an immigrant in Saudi Arabia and the United States. We were actively engaged in every process of Natsnet's asylum application process in the United States, which lasted for more than four years. We were not only developing her case and preparing her legal deposition but we also made systematic observation of her legal case and the personal struggle she was going through during her asylum ordeal. In addition to personal ethnographic narratives, we also collected an extensive literature review about Eritrean human rights issues, the history of immigration in the country from international and national human rights reports, NGO's, and peer reviewed literature. We also interviewed about 56 Eritrean asylum seekers who now live in different states in the United States to corroborate what had been witnessed and experienced by Natsnet. The interviews vary from semi-structured to unstructured interviews.

We started to write this book because we wanted to gain a better understanding of the holistic experiences of migrants. Not only what migrants' struggles look like here in the United States but also how they get here and highlight the psychological, physical, social and financial cost of the journey. In this book we attempt to document all these stories. Each chapter provides Natsnet's experience along with a deeper intellectual analysis.

Chapter 2 is a personal statement by Natsnet (the main character in the book); an Eritrean woman in her mid-30s who was born in the 1970's in Asmara, Eritrea's capital and largest city. She is the second girl in a family of many siblings. In this chapter, Natsnet presents a vivid, personal description of her home country, Eritrea, and of the familial attachment and love she experienced as a child. Her story is a personal one of growing up in a situation that would confound many people. The violence, and war that engulfed Eritrea affected her life, her family and the entire society around her. This sets the stage for the story of courage and inspiration, frustration, and determination that shaped her life as an immigrant away from home.

In Chapter 3 we present a historical and analytical profile of revolutionary Eritrea. We describe the wars with Ethiopia, and the ideologically inspired dreams of the insurgents for the "perfect" state. The religious structure of Eritrea is discussed; and the role of the Orthodox Church and other "approved" churches within Eritrean society is analyzed. The Medhane Alem Movement within the Orthodox Church is contextualized in some detail, particularly as a vehicle for building national determination in the face of overwhelming odds, as well as in the formation of Natsnet's consciousness and character. Natsnet's story is a personal ethnography involving human experiences, which are larger than just hers or Eritrea's. Local instances of human suffering, such as those she endured, often embody far-reaching global phenomena. The conflict of cultures that of thought, language, and values based on a Semitic foundation with Western thought patterns is another theme that Natsnet's ongoing story develops.

Chapter 4 focuses on Eritrea's national service obligation. We examine how the obligation works and the abuses that have been built into its operation. We finish our analysis of revolutionary Eritrea by describing its descent into dictatorship, the consolidation of power by the country's revolutionary leader, and the suppression of civil society and virtually all human rights. We explain the personal impact this had on Natsnet and other young women whom she knew and grew up with. They explain her choice what she perceived as the lesser of several evils to serve as a domestic worker abroad in one of the Gulf States, eventually choosing a Saudi Arabian family. Natsnet and her family saw this as a better choice than staying in Eritrea where she would have been conscripted into a lifelong national service.

Chapter 5 explores Natsnet's life in Saudi Arabia, "the Kingdom." While Saudi Arabia embraces a strict interpretation of Islam, the Gulf States' general views of women and people of other faiths are examined. We show that much of the normative aspects of the Gulf States' societies, and the treatment Natsnet received, are related to the similar culture countries in the region share. While slavery is formally illegal in the Gulf States, behavior patterns have remained constant, and domestic workers are treated as if they are slaves. Arab states' stereotypes of such workers are also examined. We examine all of this from a political and anthropological context, providing the normative and empirical backdrop against which Natsnet lived her life in Saudi Arabia. In so doing, the use of guest workers by the Gulf States is discussed, their living situations examined, and the world's general ignorance of their conditions presented. The role of the United States in the Gulf area is also analyzed.

In Chapter 6 Natsnet's Saudi Arabian host family plans a vacation to Orange City in the Southern part of the United States, and takes Natsnet with them. In a luxurious Southern hotel, Natsnet is beaten and abused for the last time. She escapes, knowing only that she is in America, of which she has only the vaguest knowledge. This chapter provides an analysis of the social, cultural and political forces that influenced Natsnet's escape from the Saudi Arabian family and seeking refuge in the United States. We explore, in detail, her fears of the unknown, her bravery in seeking help from strangers, and the beginning of a new life in America.

In Chapter 7 we describe Natsnet initial encounters with the American court system, which was particularly challenging given her limited knowledge of the legal system and her limitation with the English language. This chapter also describes the three faces of Eritrea (homeland, diaspora, and cyber), the Eritrean government's control of its diaspora, and the constant threat hanging over Natsnet and all diaspora Eritreans by detailing what it means being an Eritrean diaspora. This chapter shows the degree of control the Eritrean government has on its diaspora, the discussion of Eritreans politics in cyber space and social media. We also discuss the intimidation and repression people face at home because of actions of family members in the diaspora or family members who escaped from the national service and left the country.

Chapter 8 examines the immigration and political asylum process in the United States from political science and anthropological perspectives by providing detailed background information on the immigration/political asylum process, including the maze through which an asylum-seeker must navigate. This "neutral" description of "the process" is itself a telling indictment of the system. While the immigration process can be made to work, and in a vague sense is fair, access to skilled help and monetary resources are practical prerequisites. We explain the financial, communication, and cultural barriers immigrants face to obtain their legal status in the US.

In Chapter 9 we tell of Natsnet's further encounters with the American court system, much of which was brokered by author Dawit Woldu. They share their story of navigating the system's nuances, and provide their impressions of the immigration system. We find it disturbing that many attorneys' lack of knowledge of world geopolitical dynamics and cultural understanding of their clients, especially those from non-western backgrounds, in whose legal interests they work. This is placed within the context of the conflict of Western legal norms with non-western cultures, an important theme of this work.

Chapter 10 provides a detailed examination of American public opinion about illegal immigrants. The reaction to Irv Bromall's work in Moab, a small, extremely rural southeastern Utah town of 5,000, is examined. Personal bigotry against immigrants from few members of his community and the support he received is discussed. The institutionalized nature of bigotry toward immigrants is also explored. The chapter also describes the experience of Dawit Woldu while he was a resident of Gainesville, Florida, a living embodiment of the culture wars that plague the US on so many fronts. Gainesville is home to both the liberal University of Florida and the notorious and vitriolic Qur'an-burning "man of God." Like Irv, the support Dawit received and the criticism visited on him are explored in the context of ideological and social differences America faces today on immigration.

In Chapter 11, we examine the socio-economic and cultural attributes of the American political-asylum system. Basing our comments and observations primarily on our own experiences while working on Natsnet's case, and secondarily using empirical studies on the subject, we offer a critique of the system's operation and its players. We also provide detailed information about the lack of cultural competence among those in the legal system dealing with immigration cases with examples from the different encounters we had with attorneys and immigration judges.

In the concluding chapter, we return to some of the contemporary immigration issues and basic human rights violations, especially regarding women in the Middle East. We explore other similar human rights violations that are documented by other organizations. We also explore the price of justice people like Natsnet pay to get their asylum protection or other immigration benefits once they get to the United States and other developed nations.

Finally, we would like to inform our reader's the stories are modified and at times enhanced to present an Eritrean family structure, culture, and social structure rather than a direct representation of Natsnet's family. However, all the stories presented are a reflection of the social, political and cultural realities of modern Eritrea, Saudi Arabia, and the United States.

Notes

1. "A general term that refers to the movements of refugees and internally displaced people (those displaced by conflicts) as well as people displaced by natural or environmental disasters, chemical or nuclear disasters, famine, or development projects.' Forced migration Online, an NGO, views forced migration as a complex, wide-ranging and pervasive set of phenomena." (Source: http://www.forcedmigration.org/about)
2. The recruitment, transportation, transfer, harboring or receipt of persons, by means of the threat or use of force or other forms of coercion, of abduction, of fraud, of deception, of the abuse of power or of a position of vulnerability or of the giving or receiving of payments or benefits to achieve the consent of a person having control over another person, for the purpose of exploitation" (Art. 3(a), UN Protocol to Prevent, Suppress and Punish Trafficking in Persons, Especially Women and Children, Supplementing the UN Convention against Transnational Organized Crime, 2000). Trafficking in persons can take place within the borders of one State or may have a transnational character (IOM and UNHCR 2008).
3. Procurement, in order to obtain, directly or indirectly, a financial or other material benefit, of the illegal entry of a person into a State Party of which the person is not a national or a permanent resident. (Article 3 UN Convention) (IOM)
4. The kidnapping of refugees from refugee camps and taking them hostage for ransom. Once a refugee is kidnapped by traffickers they call the victim's family and ask them for a ransom. Once a ransom is paid traffickers will take the victim to certain trafficking route such as to Sanai destined to Israel or Libya destined to Europe. In the context Eritrean refugees, most of these people are kidnapped from Sudan and Ethiopian refugee camps and sometime from Eritrean border towns.

CHAPTER 2. AN OPENING LETTER FROM NATSNET: *WHY I WANT TO TELL MY STORY*

Dear Reader,

My name is Natsnet. I am an immigrant to the United States from Eritrea, a small country in northeast Africa bordering the Red Sea. I was born there in mid-1970's. My journey to America, now my home, took me from Eritrea to Saudi Arabia in mid-1990 where I worked as a domestic house servant. I was really a slave. My Saudi Arabian masters trafficked me here to the United States in early 2000's. I escaped and I have been here ever since. I want to tell you my story.

I come from a part of the world that is so different from America. Different, not just in physical things like buildings, autos, washing machines, and materialistic things of that sort, but different in a much deeper sense. Sometimes it is as if I am in a haze, a fog of time, the mist of cultures and it is hard to understand how this society works. When you are an immigrant, everything that you were and are now and so much that gives your life meaning has been erased. Can I, as a daughter of Africa, also be a daughter of America? Ever?

My family still live in Eritrea and I constantly fear what the regime might do to them if I tell my story. The American government and many others have documented its grievous crimes. Please listen to this immigrant daughter of Africa, and hope my story help you understand the life and experiences of people outside your own social and geographical borders.

This book tells of my trials during my journey from Eritrea to America. It even tells of some of my joys as when I was growing up with my family.

When I was born, Eritrea was a province of Ethiopia, not an independent nation as it is now. Haile Selassie, the emperor, had just been overthrown in a bloody coup. I experienced the never ending war for independence from Ethiopia, civil war and constant turmoil at home, and the emergence of a brutal dictatorship. Years of methodical terror, deep famine, and a dreadful life then began and continue even now for the Eritrean people, decades later. This emerging dictatorship systematically murdered its people, especially its young men, the hope of its future. During the war, a question on the lips of all was "Will it never end?" That question is still being asked. "Will it never end? Will it never end?"

After independence was declared in 1993, and I was an adolescent, the regime put in place a national service requirement for all youth to begin after high school. It was really a draft into forced labor. As a girl, I had the option of going to Saudi Arabia as a domestic worker, locally known as *kuntrat*, or doing my national service at home, most likely in the military. Accounts of other young women's experiences in the Eritrean military abounded, and they told of horrible abuse, dreadful molestation, and rape. I chose to go to Saudi Arabia, where I arrived in mid-1990. Quickly, I learned the depth of oppression to which a society can subject women! My choice, in actuality, had been between two horrendous evils – the fire or the frying pan, as the American saying goes.

I know that Saudi Arabia is America's fast friend and strategic ally, but the insights I gained into the Saudi Arabia way of thinking, acting, and behaving must be considered and thought deeply about. I have had experiences that few Americans and other westerners ever have, and I pray you never will.

In Saudi Arabia, I was confined in the home of my keepers a man, his wife, and their kids. It was a guarded compound where I was held as a virtual prisoner. I could not leave. I was abused in the most fundamental and personal ways and hurt in ways you cannot imagine. The husband sexually harassed me; the wife beat me almost every week. Even the children hit me occasionally. I was treated like their plaything, just an object, and a non-person. It seemed that this torture would never stop!

In early mid 2000's, my Saudi Arabia keepers took me with them and brought me to the United States. I was to be their slave while they were on vacation at a theme park in America. I will call that place Orange City. There, in the hotel in which I was kept along with them in their luxury quarters, she beat me for the last time. I escaped.

I was on the street, but I did not know where I was. I walked and walked, just to get away from that hotel. By pure luck, I met an Ethiopian lady on the street. She invited me to come with her, and she and her husband took me to their home which they shared with me. The couple cared for me, listened to my story, showed me sympathy, and encouraged me to seek asylum here in America. I heeded their advice.

My encounters with the American immigration bureaucracy and judicial system were ultimately a success, but also entailed years of frightful experiences. I endured setbacks and disappointments, felt plenty of frustration and pain, and experienced what I see now as wrongful and unjust treatment by the American legal system.

I was ill-served by two attorneys, out and out deceived by the second, resulting in a deportation order for perjury. It was as if the dice was always loaded against me, the cards always stacked; I could not win. Yes, there were a few high points and yes, ultimately, I was granted asylum. However, I had to pay unimaginable mental, social, and financial price to win.

My faith in Almighty God, rooted in the Orthodox Christian tradition, sustained me throughout my journey from my past to my "present." In Orange City, my pastor and congregation comforted me in my struggle, just as they nourish me now in my daily life. While I am terribly grateful to the diaspora community in my new town for helping me as best as they could, I know that in so doing they provided me a cocoon in which to hide myself. All of us tried so hard to build our lives, pretending that we were still "back home." It was as if I were still a child in Eritrea.

I lived on the edge of America, an outsider always looking in, but never an active member. In many ways, this is still my seat at the American table, the place where I taste, but do not savor American life. Here in my new town, Orange City, there is so much talk about immigration, "illegals," and "securing the borders." While I cannot understand everything, I can sense, and feel the intensity of their feelings. I am an immigrant. I am from Africa. I am black. In so many ways, I think I may fit their target for loathing, and I become frightened. Are they talking about me? Am I as hated as are the ones about whom some always talk? I hope that it will not be this way forever, but I fear for what might become of me.

Now that the asylum process is over, I can think more clearly. The more I think, the more I want my story to be told, to be known, and to serve as a lesson to others. Much of my narrative is that of an immigrant to America, navigating my way between two cultures, two sets of thought patterns, and two basic ways of "knowing." The clash of civilizations and patterns of migration and immigration are overriding themes on which my account turns.

So much of what I will tell you happened to me, an ordinary child of my country, the loved girl of a family of many children with loving and caring middle-class parents just like so many American families. I hope that you will learn from my story. Some say that mine is a tale of courage, determination, and inspiration, but that is not for me to judge.

Before I close, I want to introduce you to two of my good friends who will tell my story in the chapters to follow. I love both dearly just as I know they love me. The first is Dawit, who was of great comfort during my whole ordeal. He is now a medical anthropologist and professor, but he was a fellow refugee from Eritrea, who sought and was granted political asylum, and is now an American citizen. He was my cultural intermediary, guiding me in the ways of American society, my role model, and a cherished friend!

Dawit worked with our second friend, Dr. Irv Bromall, an American political scientist and former federal manager of Transportation and Civil Rights, who worked for many years in civil rights in Washington D.C. He was a wonderful human being, humble, and generous and I call him an angel. We lost him in March of 2014 at his home in Moab, Utah. Irv will always be in my heart. He played like a father figure for me during my asylum ordeal and he always made sure I kept hope and worked hard to reach where I am today. His material and moral support has sustained me during the most difficult days of my life. Irv's passing has been a difficult time for me and the many people he touched but I know he is in a better place, a place of joyful eternity in heaven, where a person of God like Irv is always welcomed.

Dawit and Irv's concerns focus on the structures, processes, and theoretical bases of the evil that I endured. They will share their insights, binding my story together with insights gained from their backgrounds, experiences, and study of cultural anthropology and political science, weaving their commentary in with mine. Both believe strongly that social science can point the way and guide social change.

Please read about my story and consider the opportunities America offers and the example it sets for the world. More importantly, remember those who are systematically denied those opportunities, both here and in other nations throughout the world. None of us, if we call ourselves good and virtuous, can ever forget those who are themselves forgotten by most. I want you to see things as I see them, and to think of what it means to be an immigrant woman, a daughter of Africa, a daughter of Abraham, and maybe, even someday, a daughter of America.

I hope my story evokes the goodness and wisdom that is in all our hearts. I hope it helps each of us think about how social institutions operate both in America and in the larger world. Most of all, I hope it helps all of us envision the role we all can play in making things better for those who do not sit at the table of opportunity.

Salaam,
Natsnet T'eum
Orange City
August 1, 2015

CHAPTER 3. GROWING UP IN WAR-TORN ERITREA

The Eritrea of Natsnet's Childhood

In mid-1970's, a little girl was born in Asmara, the capital and largest city in Eritrea. Lying strategically on the Red Sea in northeastern Africa, Eritrea was then an unwilling province of Ethiopia, from which it had been fighting for independence since 1961. To Eritreans, the war of liberation was a war that had to be, but seemed never to end. When it did finally end in 1991, it was the longest civil war in Africa up to that date.

Violence and fighting were very much part of the reality of all Eritreans at that time. Asmara's streets were choked with Ethiopian convoys and soldiers were everywhere. Checkpoints, manned by armed soldiers, made free movement impossible. Gunfire, skirmishes, and clandestine operations could be heard by the residents, especially at night. The Ethiopian Emperor Haile Selassie was deposed in September 1974, and Ethiopia including its Eritrean province slid into a state of ever deepening terror. The liberation movement within Eritrea itself was rent by factional disputes, often erupting in civil war.

For the most part, Asmara was spared the brunt of the conflict that plagued other parts of the country. Besides occasional pockmarks, the colonial beauty of Asmara, a "gift" left by a half century of demeaning Italian occupation, remained remarkably intact, its Art Deco styles as stunning as ever. The climate of fear and the clash of politics that prevailed in those years gave Asmara a surreal feel. Among Asmarinos, these grand structures were the touchstones of daily life.

Natsnet's grandfather, a distinguished priest in the Orthodox Church, the Reverend Father Moges, felt that his granddaughter's birth was a sign from God of a better life for all yet to come. He told the family that because of his position, and as an honor to him, he was able to arrange for the child to be baptized in the great Cathedral of *Enda Mariam* or St. Mary, in the heart of Asmara, the citadel of Eritrea's Orthodox faithful. "It was a special privilege!" he said. "*Baksheesh* works even for the clergy!" thought her mother.

Within the traditional 80 days, prescribed by the Orthodox Church, the child was named Natsnet, which in Tigrinya, a major language of Eritrea, means "Freedom." She was then baptized at the Cathedral in a traditional celebration, which recalls Jesus' baptism by John, traditionally known as the Ethiopian/Eritrean Orthodox holiday of *"Timkit."* Her chrismation or confirmation, anointing with the sacred *Chrism*, and her first communion followed.

At the baptismal ceremony, all of her extended family were there, especially her grandmother, *Abaye* Selam, whom, over the years, Natsnet grew to love with a special tenderness. Her grandfather participated in the solemn service, although he did not officiate. That honor was given to Natsnet's family's parish priest, Fr. Habab. The priest-grandfather held a serving role which he thought appropriate. Friends of the family and neighbors also joined the baptismal party.

The rite was conducted in the finest tradition of the Coptic family of churches. The officiating priest intoned the solemn service in the ancient liturgical language of the church, *Ge'ez*. Singing, chanting, incense, holy water, and three kinds of oil the most holy, the *Chrism*, fragrant with sweet spices spoke of the holy realm to the baby Natsnet and to all of those present. Just as the joyously peaceful nature of the service testified to the abstract good in humankind, the world outside of the church bore witness to humanity's opposite side. For a small interval of time and space, Natsnet's baptism obscured the chaos in which Eritrea found herself.

In the years to come, on seeing the cathedral in Asmara's center, Natsnet would remember the stories told by her family of her baptismal day. She would also remember the cathedral's two imposing towers, standing on either side of the nave. The entrance to the nave was through two massive doors that opened into the narthex, the antechamber, or entry hall to the church's massive interior. A seven panel mural had been painted over the entrance to the Cathedral, depicting the holiest people of Christianity. The cathedral's ancient "bells," looking to some like broken elephant tusks, made a pleasing ringing sound when struck with a stick-like object crafted for that purpose. Many Westerners found their sound eerie, but to Eritreans, the sound was beautiful, that of angels. The bells were rung at Natsnet's baptism when she was marked as a child of God just as her Eritrean childhood would brand her as a progeny of conflict, a true daughter of Africa.

BACKGROUND SECTION NO. 1:

A Capsule of History of Eritrea

I. From the Dawn of Time and Until the Modern Day

Eritrea to Colonial Times: Present-day Eritrea traces its roots to ancient times. Rich archaeological finds in both Eritrea and northern Ethiopia date to *ca.* 8000 B.C.E. Lucy, the three-million-old-plus *Australopithicus Afarensis* hominid (ancestor to our species), found in the Afar Triangle, is a well-known testimony to the region's antiquity. Eritrea is part of the world in which legends, myths, and stories of King Solomon and the Queen of Sheba, the sacred Ark of the Covenant, and many more abound. Eritrea was part of the fabled land of *Punt,* spoken of in 2400 B.C.E. Pharaonic Egypt. Eritrea is a land rich in antiquity and culture, with a vibrant history.

Axum, a city now in modern-day Tigray, in northern Ethiopia, developed by the first century C.E. into the Axumite Empire, a world power. Axum held sway over what is now Eritrea, northern Ethiopia, northern Sudan, and Yemen, with Adulis on the Red Sea coast of Eritrea as its main port. By the fourth century C.E., Christianity had become widely accepted.

It is believed that in the fourth century C.E., the Beja tribe, originating in what is now Sudan, occupied a good portion of the highlands and northern coast of Eritrea. Arab forces occupied coastal areas. Eritrea functioned as one of many pieces in the game of Middle Eastern politics. Gradually, the Abyssinian state, the precursor of today's Ethiopia and Eritrea, was consolidated. Many rulers led this process and it was intertwined with the growing domestic potency of the Orthodox Church. Slowly, the northeastern province of Tigray gained the upper hand in the struggle to consolidate power in the emerging Ethiopian state which itself was oftentimes more an idea than a reality. In this process, the highlands of Ethiopia and present-day Eritrea were spawning grounds of the Tigrinya-speaking ethnic groups, the long-dominant force in Eritrea, and the Amhara, paramount until recently in modern-day Ethiopia.

In the seventh century C.E., the rise of Islam and Arab political strength, the gradual extension of Islam into the Horn of Africa, and the incursions of other groups marked the beginning of Axum's decline. The Arab presence began in the coastal areas and moved into the interior as trade morphed into occupation. Initially welcomed by Axumite rulers Abyssinia was the first territory in the region to accept Muslim refugees who feared persecution in the Middle East. The growing strength of Muslim immigrants ended the hegemony of Axum's kings.

Islamic expansion was significant in many ways. First, it represented the growing complexity and diversity of the region of the Horn. Second, Islamic expansion into the Horn, and the relatively peaceful coexistence of Islam and Christianity over the centuries until today shaped the social and religious fabric of Eritrean and Ethiopian society in fundamental ways.

Over the centuries, Abyssinia grew, consolidating itself. As it grew, it began to explore the world around it, what some would call the "near abroad". In the 1300s, Abyssinians visited Rome. Later, visitors from abroad – many from Portugal – came to this fabled place and returned with stories that themselves grew to legendary proportions. Abyssinia or contemporary Ethiopia and Eritrea, in the imaginations of many, became a distant Christian land ruled by kings descending from Solomon. In the western world, Prester John and the land he ruled was a fabled myth.

In the 16th century, and continuing for three more centuries, the Turks occupied the coastal area of Eritrea. In the 19th century the Egyptians arrived taking the port city of Massawa. Short-lived Egyptian attempts to occupy the region were replaced by Ethiopia and later Italy with the scramble for Africa. In fact, the name "Eritrea" is the Italian form of a Greek term meaning "red" (land), a reference to its Red Sea location.

II. A Political Entity Emerges

Italian Control and the Emergence of Eritrea as a Political Entity: After the ten-year period of building the Suez Canal, and its opening in 1869, Italy, harboring dreams of an Italian-dominated Mediterranean Basin, showed a heightened interest in the geopolitically strategic lands of the Horn of Africa. Italy occupied Somalia, which became Italian Somaliland, an Italian colony.

Italy also schemed to assume control of Ethiopia as a protectorate, resulting in the First Italo-Ethiopian War beginning in 1885, the invasion of Ethiopia, and the humiliating defeat the Italians suffered at the hands of the Ethiopians at the Battle of Adwa in 1896. European loss at the Battle of Adwa was a defining point in the region's history. A well-armed western power with modern weapons was defeated by African warriors of an independent African state using weapons seen by Europeans as "primitive". Put more bluntly, defeat by blacks, seen by Europeans as hardly more than savages, was a hard pill to swallow in the West and a moment of great national pride for Ethiopia and the region.

In 1889, the Ethiopian Emperor Menelik accepted the Treaty of Wuchale, ending the First Italo-Ethiopian War. The treaty marked the border between a geographically reduced Ethiopia and the Italian colony of Eritrea established by the treaty on 1 January 1890. For the first time, a geographical entity, "Eritrea," was established, within whose formal, now national, borders a social and cultural system–distinct yet related to northern Ethiopia's Tigray–and political culture would evolve.

The Second Italo-Ethiopian War, begun in 1935, ended in a June 1936 Italian victory. Italy's goals were to access the resources of the Horn, obtain a strategic position on the Red Sea, and resettle Italians, mainly from the poor southern portion of Italy, especially Sicily. King Victor Emmanuel III of Italy proclaimed himself Emperor of Ethiopia and Italian control was asserted through a viceroy.

Shortly thereafter, the establishment of *Africa Orientale Italiana* (AOI) or Italian East Africa was proclaimed by Benito Mussolini in a theatrical speech in Rome as only *il Duce* could. Italian East Africa was composed of six governorates: four Ethiopian provinces, Eritrea, and Italian Somali land. In 1940, Italy joined in World War II as an Axis power. The AOI fell in April 1941, when Italian forces were defeated by the Allies. Formal control of Eritrea then passed to the United Kingdom.

British Protectorate: With Allied concurrence, the British Protectorate of Eritrea lasted from April 1941 until September 1952. The cost to Britain of maintaining its Empire and acting as a world power met head-on the financial woes it encountered after World War II. From the British perspective, shedding control of Eritrea and its transfer of control to Ethiopia made geopolitical and financial sense. When Britain left Eritrea, it took everything that could be dismantled, lifted, or packed. The Eritrean infrastructure was destroyed.

A lasting distaste for Britain remained among the emerging urban middle classes that the UK presence and its war effort had helped grow. *Shiftas* pocket groups of rebellion against established order, expanded their areas of influence. Tracing their history to medieval times in Eritrea, the *shiftas* then fought for an exploited peasantry. In contemporary times, their raîson d'être was their opposition to British rule and the status quo. In a historical sense, *shiftas* were part of the cultural *Gestalt* that spawned the Eritrean liberation movement that eventually resulted in Eritrea's independence. British expansion of the Eritrean educational system, and the western democratic ideas that it imparted to its mostly elite students, constituted the lasting contributions of the UK protectorate.

Federation with Ethiopia Followed by Annexation: The year 1952 was critical in Eritrea's history. In March, the first Eritrean Assembly was elected, and in June, a UN-drafted constitution was adopted and a chief executive elected. On 15 September, under UN guidance, and with firm US support, Eritrea was federated with Ethiopia, a feudal kingdom with a proud past stretching back to biblical times.

During federation, Ethiopian rule was harsh and Eritrea was treated as anything but a federal equal. Internal Eritrean political activity was stifled. The Eritrean Assembly became a vassal organ of Addis Ababa. Amharic, the language of Ethiopia, replaced Tigrinya and Arabic, the languages of Eritrea, as the means of instruction in the schools. The symbols of Eritrean statehood its laws and flag were replaced by Ethiopia's, and the government was officially named the "Ethiopian Administration under Haile Selassie, Emperor of Ethiopia." On 14 November 1962, the Eritrean Assembly abolished itself and the Ethiopian National Assembly in Addis Ababa abolished the federation and annexed Eritrea as the 14th province of Ethiopia. This began in earnest the 30-year war between Eritrea and Ethiopia for Eritrean independence that lasted until 1991.

The War with Ethiopia for Eritrean Independence: The politics of Eritrean liberation was rent with schisms. Not only was Ethiopia the enemy, but competing liberation factions, each fighting for the same goal, conflicted endlessly in what, in many cases, amounted to an Eritrean civil war. In September 1974, Haile Selassie was overthrown and the *Derg*, a committee of military officers that imposed Marxist rule and a reign of terror on Ethiopia, assumed and gradually consolidated power. The *Derg* broke its ties with the United States and allied itself with the Soviet Union which sent troops to Ethiopia and Eritrea in support of the *Derg*. A new player was added to the Eritrean mix.

Eritrea partly because of the evolution of its institutions and infrastructure under colonial rule was more highly developed than Ethiopia. Nascent civil institutions (e.g., an elected legislative body, the Assembly, and a UN-drafted constitution) existed as well as a rudimentary manufacturing base. Unions were developing and Eritrea's urban areas were populated with an emerging middle class. Eritrea also possessed a proud ancient history and rich culture, enhanced by its location as a "crossroads" state, an area of dynamic cultural interchange between Asia, the Arabian Peninsula, and Africa. (Henze, 2000: 273-275)

Independence: By 1991, the 30-year war for independence from Ethiopia was won and Eritrea was a de facto independent state. With UN backing, a victorious Eritrean provisional government held a referendum on independence in April of 1993. Overwhelmingly, the Eritrean electorate endorsed independence which was proclaimed on 24 May 1994. The story, from then to now, of Eritrea as an independent state will be told in other parts of this work.

Asmara During Natsnet's Growing up Years

During the January of early 1980, Natsnet celebrated her fifth birthday. Despite the horrors that enveloped Eritrea, her early remembrances of childhood are quite pleasant. She grew up with her parents, Berhane and Abrhet, and her brothers and sisters. Natsnet, the eldest of the girls in the family, was indeed spoiled by her parents! Four of her brothers were older, and two of her sisters and a brother were younger. Of all her brothers and sisters, Yohannes, born in 1980, was the closest to Natsnet. Her parents, along with Yohannes, and *Abaye* Selam, made up Natsnet's special childhood world. The family had a liquor store business and they were better off than most at that time. Despite the chaos everywhere around them, these were happy times for Natsnet at least as she recalls them now. (Note: *All names used in this section and the entire book are pseudonyms*)

The neighborhood where Natsnet and her family lived reflected the family's relatively comfortable economic status. It was composed of a few newer single family dwellings, some older Italian style homes, and traditional gated compounds, each containing several residences. Natsnet's family lived in a large masonry home in one such compound. It was surrounded by three two room stone houses and one other small one room dwelling, made of traditional mud and straw. *Abaye* Selam lived in one of the stone houses; the others were rented out. A lady, whose husband had been killed in the liberation war, lived in the one room house and often helped at Natsnet's home, doing cooking and cleaning chores for Natsnet's mother in exchange for rent.

Berhane and Abrhet were determined to give their children as rich and as happy a childhood as possible. High points of Natsnet's early memories of her life in Asmara were the regular Sunday walks to their Orthodox parish church for the weekly Divine Liturgy, almost a mystical escape from the chaos that existed around them. All would dress in traditional white Eritrean clothing woven from fine cotton thread. The women were draped, their heads wrapped in their richly embroidered *zuria.* Men wore their loose-fitting, all white *ejjetebab*. They would join their neighbors, similarly attired, with whom they would walk to church, oftentimes singing together the hymns that they all knew by heart. They tried to pretend that all was normal, but all knew that this was not the case.

Natsnet and her brothers were enrolled in private schools in Asmara where they all had tutors to help with their schoolwork, signs of the importance Berhane and Abrhet placed in education as well as their relative wealth and their aspirations for their children. Natsnet did her elementary studies at one of the elite schools in Asmara. With its large wooded campus, it was one of the best in Eritrea and a piece of the "modern," that is, the West, in the midst of an African war zone. The school offered both an academic and a religious component. The latter tended towards the Pentecostal with which Natsnet become familiar from neighbors who practiced that faith. Neither Natsnet nor her brothers and sister disappointed their parents by their respective academic performances. Natsnet especially liked her literature classes and she also excelled at math and science.

Natsnet's school, like Eritrea itself, was about evenly divided between Christians and Muslims. Natsnet's best friend at schools was Fozia whose parents owned a shop selling leather goods in Asmara's main shopping area. The two children, one an Orthodox Christian, and the other a Muslim were like sisters a sister Natsnet always loved to have. All of the students looked forward to the holy days of each faith. *Eid-Alfetir*, commemorating the end of the holy month of Ramadan, during which fasting was required, was the major Islamic holiday for which everyone waited in anticipation, just as they did for Christmas, a major Christian feast day. Both were happy festival days of special foods and gifts.

Asmara was the crossroads of Eritrea, just as Eritrea was the crossroads of Africa. Eritrea's rich past was marked in the city's various ethnic and religious groups: Christians, Muslims, and Jews lived in peace as Eritreans, as did Nubians, Yemeni, Italians, Greeks, Turks, Saudis, Sudanese, Egyptians, other Arabs, sub-Saharan Africans, and Britons. As a child, Natsnet heard all manner of languages on the streets of Asmara and knew people of many backgrounds. Eritreans themselves were of many ethnic backgrounds, the largest two, the Tigrinya and the Tigré, lived together in harmony. Natsnet was Tigrinya and Fozia, Tigréan. At home, Natsnet and

Fozia's families spoke Tigrinya. Fozia's family also spoke Arabic. Most people also knew at least a smattering of Amharic, the major language of Ethiopia.

The Scars of War

No matter how hard they tried, Berhane and Abrhet could not hide the reality of war nor the scars it had inflicted. While they tried to act as normally as possible and to provide their children with a sense of love and security, the children could only look on their city and see and sense from the tone of the adults' voices, that something was very gravely wrong. It was as if the children were able to intuit when the struggle for independence was not going well. Many people simply disappeared, victims of a growing Eritrean domestic despotism stemming from the intense competition among liberation factions as well as the repeated assaults of the Ethiopia army.

Radio broadcasts from Ethiopia chanted slogans of Ethiopian victory often naming specific liberation units that would be targeted. Quite visible on Asmara's streets were young men, many horribly maimed by battle all visible symbols of the ongoing civil war, reminders of the liberation struggle, and an admonition to all of the need for sacrifice. Later, these fighters would be revered as *yike'alo*, the ones who made Eritrean independence or, literally, "those who can do all things." Unlike their parents and the older ones, young Eritreans were eager to see their country free of Ethiopian rule. The realities, viciousness, and vicissitudes of war formed the cradle in which daily life took place.

The struggle for independence became endowed with religious fervor: it was a struggle for good, right, and the perfect society established through the perfect state. It was a prequel to the creation of an ideologically based god that could only fail! Factional strife within Eritrea, and the fight for liberation from Ethiopia, molded Natsnet's childhood and typified the environment of her growing up years. Asmara, as all of Eritrea, was on a war footing; a culture of fear prevailed. Rumor replaced news and the city teemed with confusion.

Natsnet Comes to Political Consciousness

Two incidents illustrate well Natsnet's early perceptions of war and her first conscious introduction to its horrors. The first involved the family's rare, but memorable, visits to Berhane and Abrhet's village, Mai-frdi, their *'adi'* for special occasions such as religious holidays, birthdays, weddings, extended family gatherings, and the like. The *'adi,* in the highlands, in the south near the Ethiopian border, was beautiful, located on a steep cliff overlooking the countryside. The hills and the plains below were green from September to December. Sometimes after a rainy spell, the wild sunflowers seemed to Natsnet to reach to the sky, making the entire landscape yellow. It was a place of outstanding natural beauty and peace, a sharp contrast to urban and struggle-torn Asmara!

Natsnet remembers the church in Mai-frdi. It was built in the circular style of many of the houses, all with conical roofs, found in that part of Eritrea and in neighboring Tigray Province in Ethiopia. Natsnet went there often, just to go inside and be with the spectacular artwork and icons, which sometimes seemed to talk to her. One fresco in particular, depicting Mary holding the baby Jesus, was her favorite. She dreamed that one day she might have a child to raise.

When she was very young she used to see artwork. A mural in the church's interior, painted by an Ethiopian Deacon artist, showed the Battle of Adwa where Ethiopian troops had repulsed the Italian forces. Mai-frdi was not all that far from Adwa and the people all told stories about those times. In so many ways, Eritrea was intertwined with Ethiopia in history, religion, ethnicity, familial ties, and mutual need for one another. Many in Natsnet's family had served with pride the imperial government in Addis Ababa. In all of her education, most of it dominated by an Ethiopian motif, Natsnet was taught that the Battle of Adwa was a major moment in Ethiopian history, on a plain with the coronation of Haile Selassie. At Adwa, poorly trained African forces had defeated a confident and sophisticated European power; at the coronation, the crowned heads of Europe paid homage to the Ethiopian emperor giving Ethiopia and its ruling elites the status for which they so thirsted and which had been so long denied to Africans. All those artworks are now gone replaced after Eritrean independence with religious paintings of different saints.

From a broader perspective, the Battle of Adwa was a great moment for all Africans and looking at that mural instilled in Natsnet a pride in her land that she could not explain. One of the soldiers in the mural even looked like her uncle, her *daddy*'s brother! It was one more place where Natsnet found a bit of solace, solitude, and even inspiration.

Not only does Natsnet remember Mai-frdi's beauty, but she remembers the kindness of the people there. It was a rural society at its finest and its residents showed all of Natsnet's family the bonds of an *'adi*'s heritage, the affection of a communal social order, and the deep love that comes from the hearts of those who live in tight-knit communities and work the land. Mai-frdi was a special place for Natsnet.

Once, when she was in Asmara at the family's house in the compound, Natsnet remembers longing to go to the village, a retreat from the reality of the capital. Her *dadi* said, "Sorry, my daughter, we can't go now." Natsnet asked, "Why not *Dadi*?" and Berhane, with obvious emotion, told her that the road was not safe. "There is fighting and our village is currently under heavy attack. Several of our neighbors died in the attacks: *Wayzeuro* Zahra, *Ato* Demas, and the man of God, *Sheikh* Osman.[1]" ***Natsnet***, older than her youthful years, just stared at her *dadi*, before bursting into sobs. This was Natsnet's first straightforward conversation about war and in that one instant, she realized the depth of the trouble that plagued Eritrea, and the level to which humankind could descend.

A second, even more foreboding event forever molded Natsnet's consciousness. It took place in Asmara, when Natsnet attended elementary school. During this time, she often saw Ethiopian military in Asmara. Sometimes she would see them threatening people, even making arrests for no apparent reason. At night, she could hear their gunshots from her bedroom. Ethiopian soldiers were to be feared and Natsnet knew this well, although she was never told to feel that way or knew why she knew.

One day, while Natsnet was at school, several soldiers burst into the compound, breaking the lock on the gate, and forcing their way into *Abaye* Selam's house. They accused her of hiding Eritrean rebels. Gramma was there with three of her closest lady friends who were all having lunch. *Abaye* Selam had been able to get some beef, hard to find in Asmara in those days, and had prepared *zilzil*[2] for her friends. She had spent a busy morning preparing the meal and making the *injera* to go with it.

The soldiers ordered the four women to leave the *mesob* around which they were sitting and huddle together in a corner where the trembling women were interrogated, threatened, and insulted. The soldiers shouted in Amharic that all Eritreans were "traitors to the revolution, nothing but bourgeois pigs." Then the soldiers overturned the *mesob* and the platter spread with food, ransacked the house, searching closets and cabinets, and trashing *Abaye* Selam's precious coffee service as a malicious act of destruction.

Gramma screamed in halting Amharic for the soldiers to leave, stating that none of them had done nothing wrong. The soldiers then did start to leave. One turned, sneered, and simply shot *Abaye* Selam in the head at point-blank range, killing her instantly. Then they left, swaggering out of the compound, almost as if they were proud of the act they had just committed. Today when Natsnet tells of this incident, she cries, and, remembering back to that time, says she sobbed for days, thinking her world had ended. She tells of her love for Gramma Selam and her consciousness of what Eritrea's war for independence really meant.

Perhaps it was in the wake of this last instance, or maybe it was the two events together, that Natsnet came to a newer and deeper understanding of political reality. Perhaps it was also events such as these that gave Natsnet her lifelong ability to endure formidable situations and pick up and get on with it–not only because that is what people are supposed to do, but because this is the way Eritreans do. Natsnet has carried the memories of those two moments, and of the epiphany those moments brought, throughout her life.

While Natsnet's parents, Abrhet and Berhane, may have created a very false cocoon of reality for their children, they still wanted them to grow up and do well, imagining a new Eritrea free of strife, a future that to this day has not come. It was in this domestic setting, with a growing religious faith, that Natsnet grew.

Eritrean Independence Comes

When Eritrean independence finally was assured in 1991, a referendum to confirm the victory was scheduled and took place in April 1993. The people overwhelmingly confirmed the military triumph and Eritrea was free, proclaiming its independence on 24 May 1993. The victory over Ethiopia was complete.

Independence Day was a great holiday. The new president of Eritrea, Isaias Afwerki, a valiant and charismatic *yike'alo*, spoke, expressing the dreams that all had for a peaceful, prosperous, and democratic future. Heads of state and governmental representatives from many countries were there. Even the new president of Ethiopia, acknowledging Eritrea's reality and recognizing the two countries' dependence on one another, was present to offer good wishes. The presidents were brothers in struggle, comrades in revolution, and now leaders of their respective states. For several years, Ethiopia and an independent Eritrea did live in a cooperative and peaceful fashion.

After the speech, it seemed as if all of Asmara exploded in celebration. Natsnet's brothers ran from the compound and into the city; Natsnet's parents, ever protective of their daughter, kept her home. However, Natsnet remembers people thronging into the streets to celebrate. Every avenue, every alley, was massed with joyous people. Eritrea liberation fighters were embraced, kissed on their cheeks over and over, lifted on the shoulders of the crowd, and lauded as saviors of the nation as, in truth, they certainly were! Everyone was waving Eritrean flags, ringing bells, beating pans, or making noise with anything they could find. She heard ululation the "joyful noise" the Bible speaks about from every side of the city.

Natsnet heard of people testifying of their struggles and of the great victory now won. Some even proclaimed that the Promised Land had come. Others just jumped and screamed for joy. Everywhere, in every corner of the city, patriotic songs were sung, especially the beloved songs from the liberation struggle. *"Erta, Erta, Erta,"* soon to become the national anthem, was sung again and again! The entire day was a eucharist of celebration and thanksgiving!

People stayed in the streets throughout the night. Later, when Natsnet was with her friends, they all expressed their happiness that Eritrea was free from Ethiopia's grip. It was independent! That Natsnet, now in her late teens, grasped the significance of this day indicated that she had absorbed much more of the political reality that surrounded her growing-up years than anyone thought.

In the Years to Come . . .

Nowhere in Asmara that night did any one imagine the future that was to come. The high hopes and dreams that were expressed in celebration, and the sacrifices of thousands of people like Natsnet, her family, and so many others, would soon be crushed. The imagined Eritrea of Natsnet's childhood quickly morphed into a brutal dictatorship built on those hopes and dreams. Hope for democracy was the first victim of the post-independence government.

A widely praised, but never implemented, "model" constitution, ratified by the National Assembly in 1997, remains even today unimplemented (UN Report of the Commission of Inquiry on Human Rights in Eritrea, 2015). Basic civil liberties and rights were never made real; freedom of speech and all other forms of civil rights have been deferred indefinitely (US State Department 2002-2014, UN Report of the Commission of Inquiry on Human Rights in Eritrea, 2015). Political prisoners and journalists have been thrown into high-security, secret prisons without trial. There, many disappear, languish, and die. It is a state in which the omnipresent security police, under the direct command of the executive body systematically, abuses, tortures, and kill with no consequence and accountability (UN Report of the Commission of Inquiry on Human Rights in Eritrea, 2015). As the report put it "it is a rule by fear not law". Families of alleged offenders share in the "wrongdoer's" guilt.

The national-service requirement enacted shortly after independence has made conscripted hostages of the majority of its young citizens for much of their lives (Kibreab 2009, Dorman 2005). Its second generation of youth after the revolution serve in never-ending national service against their will.

Freedom of religion has come under increasing scrutiny. Only sanctioned religious groups are free to practice their religious beliefs. (These are the Orthodox Church, Sunni Muslims, a Protestant federation with a Lutheran bent, and eastern-rite Catholics.) Small sects, defined by the Eritrean government as contrary to Eritrean culture and traditions, have been targeted (US State Department 2011-2014).

In the early years after independence, the government targeted Jehovah's Witnesses and few minority Islamic groups such as the Wahhabi sect for persecution (Dorman 2005, Human Right Watch 2008-2014). However, many other minority Christian groups now are falling victim to Eritrean governmental harassment (US State Department 2011-2014, Human Right Watch 2013, and Amnesty International 2014). Pentecostal groups "*pentes*," as they are known in what is almost a pejorative term provoke the wrath of the government. Even the historically influential Eritrean Orthodox Church, recently fell victim to the government, its patriarch deposed and held incommunicado in a location kept secret. Reformist or revivalist groups within the Orthodox Church, such as the Medhane Alem Movement, have been a special target. (In a subsequent chapter we will examine this movement since it is the source of inspiration as Natsnet's story continues.)

Like its neighbors Eritrea is also a country where female genital mutilation remains common and discrimination against women, homosexuals, and persons with HIV/AIDS is widespread (ACCORD International 2004). This is not the state that was fought for by so many brave Eritrean patriots during the terrible 30-year war for liberation with Ethiopia, finally won in 1991; and boldly proclaimed independent in 1993. The idealistic ideological constructs of the revolutionary years were dashed and a one party state was installed controlling all aspects of the country's social, economic, and political life (Abraha 2010).

On the economic front, Eritrea increasingly became anti-free market and closed (or forced to close) major privately owned businesses (Abraha 2010, Dorman 2005). On the international scene, the country quickly turned into a diplomatic disaster after independence, warring with its neighbors and the international community standing firm on its "Self-reliance" and isolationist stance (Human Right Watch 2009, Nur 2013, Reid, 2005). The Eritrean government also waged a war against the nongovernmental organizations whose purpose was to help the Eritrean people. The temporary alliance with Ethiopia would falter and the transient period of cooperation with Ethiopia morphed into an internecine war between the two states border issues as pretext (Reid 2005). Hatred for Ethiopians in Eritrea and hatred for Eritreans in Ethiopia was fueled by both governments forceful deportation of people from their respective countries (Human Right Watch 2003). Most of them were deported to Eritrea from Ethiopian leaving their property and, sometimes, loved ones behind. The Eritrean government continue to cast Ethiopia as the arch devil and the United States as Ethiopia's puppet master.

The Ethiopian and Eritrean leaders, who had joined hands at the independence celebration in Asmara in 1993, and finally fought a devastating war from 1997-2000 that had major political, economic, and social implication to the Eritrean state (Reid 2005). The Ethiopian leader lasted until his death in 2012, and the Eritrean leader lasts even to this day. Each strove to maximize his clout at the expense of the other. The very aspirations that brought Eritrea into being would be damned.

Major western governmental agencies established to promote human rights and religious freedom have condemned Eritrea's policies and practices as have major NGOs (Amnesty International 2004-2014, Human Right Watch 2014, Reporters Without Borders 2002-2014, United Nationals Human Right Council 2014). In return, Eritrea has become increasingly intolerant of criticism by western governments of its human rights posture, political stance, and repressive economic policies. Foreign assessments of civil liberties, political freedom, and religious freedom place Eritrea in the bottom-most rungs of their analytical ladders (Human Right Watch 2014, Amnesty International 2008-2014, US State Department 2011-2014).

A country that many hoped would become a prosperous democratic nation has become a source of major social, economic, and political crisis. Natsnet's hopes and her vision of an independent, free, and prosperous Eritrea of her young days is now just a dream from the past, betrayed by the horrible reality of today by the Eritrea that she loves the most.

Notes

1. In Tigrinya, *Ato* is the generic equivalent of the honorific Mr. or Sir. *Sheikh* is a religious title, generally equivalent to Reverend, used for addressing a Muslim man who holds a spiritual office. *Wayzeuro* is the honorific term for Mrs., and *Wayzeurit* for Miss
2. Tender strips of red meat cooked with red onion and jalapenos

3. *Authors' note: In this section, we try to establish a general sense a word picture, sometimes enhanced of the times, and not a complete history. We base this on our in-depth interviews with Natsnet, our reconstruction of her life's story, on other interviews with homeland and diaspora Eritreans who directly experienced this period in Eritrea's history, and on asylum declarations of several Eritreans as well as of the lead author's own experiences in Eritrea.

CHAPTER 4. NATIONAL SERVICE, NATSNET, AND HER DECISION TO GO TO SAUDI ARABIA

Eritrea's National Service Obligation

The obligation of youth to serve the state through national service was initially established by the Eritrean provisional government in 1991 and ratified by the newly independent government in 1994 by Proclamation 82. As originally written, Eritreans, between the ages of 18 and 40, were required to give 18 months of national service: 6 months of military training and 1 year's military service.

Beginning in 1994, the six-month term of military training began to take place in a central location in the western lowlands, Sawa[1], near the Sudanese border. Sawa was characterized by strict military discipline, Spartan living conditions, and a particularly brutal climate. This training essentially replaced the last year of high school, grade 12, and was a prerequisite for future advancement in Eritrean society.

Politically, Eritrea was in its first years of state consolidation. The liberation war had been won, and the new state had declared its independence. The Eritrean People's Liberation Front (EPLF), the revolution's guiding force, morphed into the Peoples Front for Democracy and Justice (PFDJ), Eritrea's sole party, sharing ideological bonds with the revolutionary regime in Ethiopia, itself dominated by Eritrea's highland neighbors from Tigray province. As the PFDJ consolidated its power, it strayed from its democratic ideals, actively pursuing policies of oppression and subjugation (Abraha 2010, Nur 2013). The state was asserting its control over all aspects of its citizens' lives, building and deploying an internal security force to monitor movement and speech. Punishment for non-compliance with the regime's wishes was swift and harsh (Bozzini 2011, UN Report of the Commission of Inquiry on Human Rights in Eritrea, 2015, Human Right Watch 2009). Citizens quickly learned that the course of least resistance was compliance with the regime's directives. The national service mandate became an important tool in the regime's consolidation of absolute power over the citizenry.

The mandate was modified on several occasions, especially after the bitter 1998-2000 border war with Ethiopia, by broadening the conscript base, raising the upper age limit for service, and making the term of service indefinite. It was not unusual to find grandfathers and their grandsons serving in national service at the same time. What was initially presented and generally accepted by the Eritrean people as a reasonable tool for rebuilding the homeland, and for its development in the wake of the 30-year war for liberation, became an instrument to create and maintain a coerced labor force for an indefinite period of service both at home and for use at least as a threat against Eritrea's Red Sea neighbors.[2]

Recently the Eritrean regime attempted to trick the international community and its own people by circulating rumors or privately telling diplomats that they will shorten the national service to 18 months. However, in reality national service continued to be the main practice holding hundreds of thousands of young and middle age people in the trenches. The Eritrean regime continue to blame the situation to the refusal of Ethiopia to implement the Algier's agreement and leave Eritrean territory. The defiance of Ethiopia not to implement the final and binding agreement of the border conflict somehow helps the Eritrean regime to get some sympathy from a significant number of Eritreans. Nevertheless, almost all Eritreans do not accept the absolute disregard of human right, endless national service, and complete disregard to the rule of law by the Eritrean regime.

National Service Work

Most women like Natsnet were assigned to government offices and facilities throughout Eritrea. Many worked directly for military officers and were expected to satisfy their needs. Many young men were assigned to laboring positions (e.g., road crews, and the like). The lucky few "lucky" in a relative sense were assigned to private businesses, government offices, schools, or to laboring positions. Many became essentially indentured servants of the emerging elite groupings in post-liberation Eritrean society. In the end, the low wages and labor benefited the PFDJ officials, high-ranking military officer corps, and the secret police, the enforcer of the regime's wishes. This was a far cry from the reconstruction of the country that the program was initially supposed to accomplish. The hopes and dreams of at least three generations of Eritreans were smashed like glass by the national service program.

The Context of Natsnet's National Service Decision

When Natsnet approached the time for national service; she was in the 11th grade and in her late teens. Finishing high school in the mid-1990s, Natsnet was eligible for national service. However, she was she was forced to choose either to go into military service or go to Saudi Arabia to work as a domestic worker. It is at this juncture that Natsnet's journey to Saudi Arabia began. The Eritrean government controls most of those migration to Saudi Arabia and other foreign countries through strict exit visa restrictions. Most of the domestic work permits in mid-1990 were reserved for women who finished their national service or women who were demobilized from the army, mostly former rebel fighters who were not needed by the Army. However, the Eritrean government changes the conditions of national service and other restrictions frequently to fit the need of the moment. For example, in early 2000s after the war with Ethiopia, the Eritrean government allowed national service age men and women with special skills to work in the private sector and the private sector to deposit the salary of these individuals in the government coffers. This decision was made to alleviate the financial pressure the government faced after the war. Dawit, the lead author in this manuscript, worked at the University of Asmara as a faculty member but his salary was paid to the government and he had to live the three years with less than $10 a month salary.

Natsnet was fortunate to learn from compatriots who went to the national service before her, the gravity of the military abuse against women. Going to the army was seen as going to hell, especially for a woman. Many of her neighbors in Asmara who had been in the army told her how they had been sexually assaulted and abused by military officers. Natsnet herself knew a handful of young girls in Asmara who had been raped in the army and become pregnant. Those who had been to Sawa told grizzly tales of sexual humiliation and abuse. Thousands of girls were sent there every six months and, when they returned, they told their stories.

The experiences of one of Natsnet's friends stood out. She was a friend from childhood, a neighbor girl, who was raped at Sawa, bore a child, and was living with her parents. Having a child out of wedlock was a terrible offence in Eritrean culture and the victims of this act were the ones who, in fact, were blamed. Her mother often came to Natsnet's house, telling Natsnet's mother how the family felt disgraced and ashamed.

The shame lay on the family and the mother in particular for not properly teaching her daughter; the girl who herself was raped; her "illegitimate" child, the product of the rape. The military officers who abused and raped the girl felt no shame and society had no power to even question the injustices the regime and the whole system inflict on its citizens. This girl's story, and other horrifying accounts, forced Natsnet to choose the lesser of two evils and to opt to join the "maid trade" in Saudi Arabia.

In making this decision, Natsnet was supported by her family and friends. As her confidence in the regime waned, Natsnet came to realize that the whole idea of national service was part of an oppressive ideology, a social engineering of creating a submissive society, to support the government. She saw her decision to go to Saudi Arabia as driven by the government, saying, "I loved my family and I am a loved daughter. It was not a nice choice, either for me or for my parents. It was just a bad situation."

The Regime's Motives: The provision of workers like Natsnet to Saudi Arabia a source of cheap labor on which the Saudi Arabian economy is dependent, was made under a contract between the Eritrean government and Saudi Arabian government affiliated companies, an employment agency, to supply such labor to Saudi Arabia. As part of the agreement between the Eritrean government and the companies, substantial portions of the wages of domestics' hired under the program were remitted to the Eritrean government. This money was collected by a diplomatic representative posted to the Eritrean Embassy in Riyadh. From the government's point of view, this was a sure source of income on top of, and in addition to, the usual two percent diaspora tax, as well as other levies, that Eritreans living abroad were expected to pay. As a condition of Natsnet's employment in Saudi Arabia and this was, in reality, an only thinly disguised state of involuntary servitude Natsnet signed an agreement to return to Eritrea when her job ended at some unspecified point in the future.

The economics of the arrangement were simple. Like many other young Eritrean women, Natsnet was encouraged by the government to seek work abroad, away from the growing economic destitution that characterized Eritrea today. From the regime's point of view this was a rationale strategy: such persons are worth more out of Eritrea than at home. The regime saw Natsnet, and others like her, as an economic commodity to be used to generate capital. Abroad, she would be a source of income for the regime, remitting a substantial portion of her wages to the government, paying her two-percent tax plus other impositions, as well as being the proverbial one less mouth to feed. The Eritrean government thus had a real incentive to impose exile on its citizens and the contract under which Natsnet was sent to Saudi Arabia was a worthwhile investment from the regime's perspective.

Natsnet's Decision: After much prayer and soul searching, Natsnet made her decision to go to Saudi Arabia to fulfill her obligation working as a domestic paying what the Eritrean government requires and hopefully saving some money for herself and her family back home. In so doing she left Eritrea in Mid 1990's, the only home she had ever known, to begin a new life in Saudi Arabia as a migrant worker with a domestic/nanny position, working for upper class Saudi Arabian family a husband and wife and their children.

Natsnet describes her decision to go to Saudi Arabia as follows:

> I never thought in my entire life I would leave my home and family and go to another country, not alone to Saudi Arabia. It was one of the toughest decisions I had to make in my life. I cried in my bed for a week leading up to my departure. I heard so many bad stories about working in Saudi Arabia but my family and I decided it would be better to go to Saudi Arabia than to Sawa. I was just scared of so many unknowns and knows about a country that so many young women do not have a fond memory. I just thought I will be going until things get better at home and the government national service project is stopped. I saw the sadness of my parents and siblings in their face and I started to comprehend what this means to me and the people I loved most, my parents and siblings. I started to realize life will not be the same for us and I was quite right. My life has changed forever because of my decision to go to Saudi Arabia. I am not the same anymore, the happy life, the joy of family, the company of friends and the beautiful people and city I grew

up are now the things of the past. I hope I will have a second chance to see that and show my kids.

Notes

1. A military training site in Southwestern Eritrea, where national service members get their military training before they are assigned to military units.
2. See especially Gaim Kibreab. "Forced labour in Eritrea." *Journal of Modern African Studies*, Vol. 47, No. 1 (2009), pp. 41-72.

CHAPTER 5. LIFE FOR NATSNET IN SAUDI ARABIA

Natsnet's new home in Saudi Arabia was a walled and guarded compound in Riyadh, the home of her "masters," a formally monogamous couple, with children. By contracting employment in Saudi Arabia, she joined thousands of other Eritrean women shipped there (Thiollet 2007). According to Thiollet's very conservative estimate, there are more than 100,000 Eritrean migrants in Saudi Arabia by 2007. This study does not specify what percentage of these migrants are actually female domestic workers like Natsnet. However, given that it is usually difficult for a male Eritrean to leave the country legally because of the extended national service requirements which a female Eritrean can avoid once she has a baby. The second reason the Saudi Arabia job market in Ethiopia and Eritrea is focused on female domestic workers. Therefore, it is likely at least more than 50% of these immigrants are female in the domestic trade. Based on our interviews "contractors" and agents in both countries process mainly female domestic workers visa cases or forced labor through trafficking (Ant-Slavery international 2006). Most of the female trade on the Eritrean side is done on Eritrean government-run "contracts" in collaboration with Saudi Arabian companies that manage those contracts locally known in Saudi Arabia as *"kafala"*. *Kafala* is a visa sponsorship and contract program that is signed between the domestic worker and the employer. In practice, the contract favors the employer and puts the domestic worker at the mercy of the employer (Mowbray 2003).

The Maid Trade

In the previous chapter we have seen the economics of Natsnet's situation from the point of view of the Eritrean government. Let us look at the larger picture, the "maid trade," which involves more than just Saudi Arabia and Eritrea. It links a web of sending countries like Eritrea, Ethiopia, the Philippines, Indonesia, Sudan, Yemen and India, with the Gulf States, that is Saudi Arabia, Bahrain, Kuwait, Oman, Qatar, and the United Arab Emirates. The national cultures of the Gulf share certain common characteristics. In each, Islamic values are the norm. Each is characterized by a patriarchal social structure with clearly delineated gender roles; and slavery, now illegal, is very much continued under other forms and guises (Anti-Slavery international 2006). Non-Arabs do constitute a numerical majority, but economic underclass, doing much of the work. A common Arab ethnic identity and Islamic faith, and concomitant sense of male supremacy, unite the individual states. From a Western perspective, norms of democratic process are missing and male chauvinism and lack of religious tolerance as the main cultural and political differences between Saudi Arabia and the west (Moaddel, 2006).

While still in Eritrea, Natsnet had heard stories that the oil rich kingdom acted with great hostility towards domestics like herself, but her life soon became much harder than she ever expected. Living there in Saudi Arabia was absolutely miserable and without legal protection or personal support. She was treated like a slave and subjected to physical, mental, and sexual abuse.

Natsnet had no support mechanisms while in Saudi Arabia, either from her own government, which saw her as an income generator, or from any institutional structures in Saudi Arabia society. Established structures such as public and private to protect immigrants are simply nonexistent for both males and females. Just as the royal family holds absolute political power, so the system provides unlimited power to maid owners/employers to do whatever they want with the person. Furthermore, the Eritrean diplomatic outposts in Saudi Arabia see these women as a source of income and do not care about the welfare of the young women sent to endure systematic human exploitation (Anti-Slavery International 2006). The international community, particularly the United States, has failed to address the plight of women in Saudi Arabia. America's strong economic, political, and security ties with the Saudi Arabian government overshadow the human rights abuse of domestic workers.

Natsnet faced unimaginable challenges, having little control over her life, and no help from her home country and the international community. Her life was in the hands of her masters and she had only herself and her faith to lift up her spirit in the face of all odds.

Natsnet's Challenges

Natsnet remembers all of the abuse she encountered both from the wife, the children, and the husband. Her life was one of indentured servitude and sexual and physical abuse suffered at the hands of the Saudi Arabian family. Each family member gave orders to Natsnet, expecting their needs to be fulfilled at lightning speed and done with a high degree of perfection. For the wife, always suspicious of her maid's motives, she was scheming to seduce her husband and possible wreck her marriage. For the husband she was a sexual object and a domestic slave. The children joined in without restraint. Any resistance from Natsnet was responded to with extreme violence and physical beating. In her affidavit describing the guarded compound to which she was confined and could not escape, Natsnet swore in her asylum deposition:

> Let me explain one of the many abuses I endured during my stay with the Saudi Arabian upper class family. I was working for an upper class family constituting of the husband, wife and their children. One day the wife went to Jeddah (Saudi' Arabia's capital city) from Riyadh, their home city and where I was working for them as a domestic worker. The night she left he came to my bedroom and sexually harassed me. I cried all night and no one was there to help me. Things were to get even worse, his wife questioned me after her return to Riyadh. She interrogated me about whether I had sex with her husband. As usual, she hit me and insulted me. She warned me not to have any affair with her husband. I wanted to leave the house, but the house is guarded with security guards and I had no freedom to go out of the house. One day I attempted to escape, however, I was caught by the guard and the husband put me in a dark room for three straight days.

> The confinement was the worst thing that ever had happened in my life. I never saw a prison, but this was a prison for me. The husband started insulting me calling me names using profanity and continued with verbal abuse such as "What do you want to do? You are out of control." He spat at me. I was crying and refused to answer his questions. He asked me why I was refusing his orders. He told me I should not complain. He said, "This is Saudi Arabia and you are a woman and a Christian. You should serve a man, your master and that is me. If you do not do that, you will face the same punishment next time."

Natsnet describes her life in Saudi Arabia in more detail as follows:

> When I first arrived in Saudi Arabia in mid-1990s I felt I was in prison. I was working 16 hours a day without break. The worst part is sometimes the husband come to me and harassed me sexually. Occasionally, I had sleep deprivation and became so tedious the whole day. His wife was so abusive. I was constantly hit by her for some household-related reason. One day she pushed me and I fell to the ground. I hurt my legs, and for days I had a lot of pain. It was a horrible life and sometimes I felt suicidal. I was not able to stand it, especially the days before I came to the United States.

Overall, for Natsnet, Saudi Arabia was a terrifying prison, and the family house a notorious cell.

Working and living conditions for domestic workers in Saudi Arabia are deplorable. In the statement summarizing its 2004 report, "Bad Dreams: Exploitation and Abuse of Migrant Workers in Saudi Arabia," Human Rights Watch stated:

> Many women employed as domestic workers in cities throughout the kingdom reported that they worked twelve hours or more daily. Most of them also lived in around-the-clock confinement, at the decision of their private employers, cut off from the outside world.... [A domestic] said that she constantly watched the locked front gate of the house, waiting for an opportunity to escape after her male employer raped her ....

In "Contract Enslavement of Female Migrant Domestic Workers in Saudi Arabia and the United Arab Emirates" in the May 2008 journal, *Human Rights & Human Welfare*, the author states, "[r]elying on employment agencies and brokers, migrant domestic workers enter contractual bondage with employers whom they have never met before, leaving themselves vulnerable to abuse and exploitation." The author continues: "[because slavery is illegal, slave-holders often use contracts as a means to legitimate and disguise the practice." What follows in the article is a thoroughly analytical description of the horrors endured by such migrant workers in Saudi Arabia (and in the United Arab Emirates). Such was Natsnet's condition of servitude.

BACKGROUND SECTION NO. 2

A Typical Work Day for Natsnet in Saudi Arabia

5:00 a.m.: Rise

5:30 a.m.: Prepare breakfast for the family

6:00 a.m.: Wake the children; serve breakfast; clean up the kitchen

7:00 a.m.: Begin washing and ironing clothes; make the beds; clean the house

9:00 a.m.: Do incidental chores; accompany the wife to the market; carry groceries and other assorted purchases

11:00 a.m.:Prepare and serve lunch for the couple; clean up the kitchen; do any needed food-preparation work

1:00 p.m.: Finish washing and ironing

2:30 p.m.: Do special chores for the wife (e.g., set up for lady friends' visit; serve snacks, tea, and assorted pastries; clean the living room after guests have left; set up the study for the children's weekly English tutorial)

5:00 p.m.: Do chores as directed by the wife

6:30 p.m.: Prepare dinner for the family

8:30 p.m.: Serve dinner; clean up the kitchen

9:00 p.m.: Give the children baths; put to bed

10: 00 p.m.: Finish up remaining chores; do other chores as directed by the wife

11:00 p.m.:Go to room to try to sleep

Natsnet had no idea about the terms of the agreement negotiated by the Eritrean government or their affiliates to supply domestic workers to individual Gulf States, and even if written statements exist, they are irrelevant once the master is given charge of the domestic worker. Life for these domestic workers is as bad as slavery with little chance to escape or for anyone to voice concern. This is the life of millions of domestic workers in the Gulf, a large desert that consumes the lives of so many domestic workers. Again, as Natsnet's case shows, the abuse of domestic workers comes from all members of the host family, children included, and it is often accompanied by violence and racial slurs and epitaphs.

Culture of Saudi Arabia

Saudi Arabia is a country and society in which women are ruled by men through well-established guardianship laws. It is a very religious based society and a system of governance in which other perspectives and ways of life are at times considered *"haram."* an Arabic term used to distance and reject the influence of non-Arabic and non-Islamic ways of life. It is a culture that has less tolerance for other ideas and religious practice (Doumato 1992). Women do not have freedom of movement; they cannot drive. They do not have equal inheritance rights to their male counterparts. The guardianship laws give absolute power to a husband, a father, or any senior male family member to make whatever decisions necessary over the women "under" him.

Natsnet states forcefully that "Saudi Arabian women do not have any single freedom; they are frustrated with the system, and the only way they can defuse their anger and frustration is on us, domestic workers." She continues "in fact, the women are more abusing and violent than men, because they are always around the house, and they could create any reason to beat a servant up." Saudi Arabia is a society with an institutionalized chain of social structure where the monarchy family is at the top (Doumato 1992). The power of the Royal family is absolute; the law rarely applies to them and the law itself is designed to protect them and expand their influence on everyone who lives in the Kingdom. Ordinary Saudi Arabians thus don't possess much power compared to members of the royal family. Men, because of the guardianship laws, have dominion over women. At the bottom of the chain of abuse and oppression are immigrants, migrant workers, especially domestics, for whom the difference between slavery and domestic worker is blurry. The treatment of domestic workers and other immigrants in Saudi Arabia is contrary to western democratic values.

Saudi Arabia and other oil-rich Gulf states are the only part of the world in which a large portion of their societies are migrant workers. However, the concept of multiculturalism is absent. Saudi Arabia hosts millions of migrant workers from Asia, particularly from the Philippines, Indonesia, India, Pakistan, and Bangladesh and from different parts of Africa particularly the Horn and northwest Africa. However, other cultures and beliefs are not respected; most of the time looked down upon and punished. There is no freedom of religion, and peaceful rites of faiths other than Islam are often broken up, and the participants punished, even when these services take place in private homes (Christian Solidarity Worldwide, 2011). In this, the Saudi Arabian *mutaween*, the religious police, play a significant role.

For example, Christian Solidarity Worldwide and an Irish based "Church in Chains", an NGO, reported in 2011 a young Eritrean man was given death sentence because of his religious practice in Saudi Arabia. Church in Chains also reported in 2013 that a group of Ethiopian Christians were rounded up from a private house and arrested because they practiced their faith. Any laws that might, even remotely, offer protections to migrant workers are not enforced. A Saudi Arabian citizen even has the power and ability to block systematically a court hearing for a case involving the individual Saudis and a migrant or domestic worker, and to have the offending person deported before the court appearance. Abuse and torture that happen within a household stay within that household. One former American English teacher for a Saudi

Arabian family described the plight of women and domestic workers in the Kingdom nation as "a country of masters and slaves" in which women are kept behind the screen and blocked from everyday life.

This is the social and political landscape that Natsnet had to navigate to survive and make a living. It is a very difficult cultural and social terrain to which she simply was unaccustomed. The kind of violence and torture she encountered is something she never imagined while growing up in a humble middle class family in Eritrea. From her masters' window, Natsnet saw so many people from Asia, Africa, Europe, and America passing by, but as a prisoner in her masters' house, she knew nothing about them. Natsnet would have loved to have known the experiences of a Filipino woman who was working with another family in the kingdom as a domestic worker in the neighborhood, or the Bangladesh driver who took the kids to school from her masters' house, or the American English teacher who tutored the kids on weekends. Natsnet's position as a virtual slave isolated her and prevented her from interacting with people other than "her" family. The social and legal rules in the kingdom made it very hard if not impossible for people like Natsnet to experience a happy life and tell their stories and suffering to people who could possibly help them.

The West Looks at Saudi Arabia

In only very few instances are people like Natsnet ever viewed as subjects of concern to the international community, particularly the West. We hear murmurings from the west sometimes, but in most cases the human rights abuse in the kingdom are overshadowed by the West's strong political, strategic, and economic relationship and its economic dependency as a major source of petroleum.

From the American perspective, encouraging the Saudis to take human rights seriously is a difficult challenge. Saudi Arabia's social and political culture militate against what is considered by the West as human right such as women's right and religious freedom (US State Department Country Report 2004, 2006). US State Department 2004 report put Saudi Arabia as a "country of special concern' when it comes to religious freedom (US State Department 2004). The US State Department country report from 2006 indicated Saudi Arabia's human rights condition continues to be poor. An Ethiopian expatriate and businessman who worked in Saudi Arabia said "In Saudi Arabia human right is not part of the discussion, the government does not even attempt to pretend to defend itself on those accusations." Despite annual US State department poor human right record of the kingdom, talking forthrightly to the Saudis would mean losing the American lifeline to oil. Furthermore, the security and political stability role Saudi Arabian government plays in the region could be in danger. The international community faces a real conundrum with the country that has so much to offer to the world economy; as its major source of oil; socially, as the birth place of one of the great religions of the world, Islam; and as a strong ally in the fight against terrorism. However, a country with a social fabric that goes against most of the cultural, political, and social values held by the West is discomforting.

Most human rights activists in the West have been voicing their concern over the Saudi Arabian government's attack on multiculturalism, denial of the rights of women, and the appalling living conditions of migrant workers. Therefore, the international community faces a major challenge to address human rights concerns and not to offend a major ally by pushing the button too hard. Moreover, Saudi Arabia cannot just be forced to make changes in the country's legal system to address the rights of women and domestic workers.

As the world is changing, especially in the face of the Arab Spring, Saudi Arabia remains defiant, continuing to maintain one of the most repressive of social orders, rejecting any value formulations that do not adhere to the Saudi Arabia form of Arabism and Islamic practice. However, how long the oppression of women and migrant workers will continue is not certain, as there is a growing demand for equality and justice by citizens throughout the world. On the other hand, we hope reform and a broader acceptance of immigrants and women's rights in Saudi Arabia will happen sooner than supporters of the status quo expect.

BACKGROUND NO. 3

Saudi Arabia Culture and History

Saudi Arabia as a kingdom was founded in 1932, however, settled agricultural communities have lived along with Bedouin nomadic tribes for at least 6000 years (Maisel and Shoup 2009:60-61; Long 2005:1). The country occupies 80% of the Arabia peninsula and it is almost one fifth the size of the United States. Saudi Arabian culture is a product of thousands of years of interaction between the Arabian peoples, their desert environment and other cultures around them. Long (2005) argues that the introduction of Islamic culture and values in the 7th century and the desert environment characterized the social, economic, political dynamics of the country. Long further argued despite its ancient history, most of the major social changes is attributed in the last 70 years with rapid oil boom that opened up the country to the outside world with improved technology and transportation systems.

However, the introduction of Islam to the Arabian Peninsula in the early 7th century is the most momentous single event in the evolution of Saudi Arabian culture (Long 2005:18). Islam introduced a very solid set of moral and socio-cultural values that have dominated the cultural and social fabric of the region until this day. More than just a religion Islam is all-encompassing and has cosmic scope. It teaches that all things animate and inanimate are God's creation and all are under God's dominion. Contemporary Saudi Arabia is shaped by Islam and Islamic laws carry on the legacy of the religion and its influence on the lives of its millions of inhabitants.

The evolution of traditional Saudi Arabian cuisine and dress, as with the Saudi culture in general, began with the indigenous people adapting to their environment. The hot, arid climate limited available food resources and called for loose, flowing garment under which air could flow (Long 2005:55). Saudi Arabian dress is mostly dictated by an Islamic dress code that emphasizes modesty with women veiling their faces and covering their entire body from the public eye. One of the earliest pre-islamic Arabian forms of dress was *Izar*, a large sheet of cloth worn either like a mantle or a sarong wrapped around the waist. A sarong-like men's garment, called *wizra* or *futah*, can still be seen in south western Saudi Arabia. Today as part of the ritual dress required in making the *Hajj*, male pilgrims to Makkah wear similar, seamless garments wrapped around their waist and another one draped over their shoulder. After the introduction of Islam Arabia dress evolved in to include five categories for men as well as women: basic attire, which consisted of long body shirts with long sleeves: undergarments for the upper body and lower body; outer garments, which consisted mainly of long, seamless robes; headwear, including headscarves and women's veils and face masks; and footwear, including shoes, slippers and sandals (Long 2005:55).

Saudi Arabia food is very much influenced by several cultures such as Egyptian, Syrian, Turkish, Indian, Indonesian, and central Asian but today they are assimilated into the Saudi Arabian Cuisine and many Saudis do not think their dishes derived from any foreign influence (Maisel and Shoup 2009:87).

In the early social formation in prehistoric time, many sedentary farmers in the oasis villages and towns grew grain notably wheat and barley and vegetables, in small garden plots and tended their date groves. Semi-nomadic sheepherders provided meat and cheese from their flocks of sheep and goats, which they herded out in the desert in the winter and then grew vegetables and food grains in the spring (Long 2005:48; Maisel and Shoup 2009:88). Nomadic Bedouin herders provided camel meat to several Saudi Arabia communities. Fresh fish was stable on the coast. Many other food ingredients such as tea, spices, coffee, and rice were imported from other countries such as Southwestern Yemen, Ethiopia and other Gulf countries which played a big role in the development of Saudi Arabia traditional food (Long 2005:48).

Contemporary Saudi Arabian culture and society is very much linked to the sanctioned religiosity and Arabism that defined the kingdom since the adoption of Islam. Much of Saudi Arabian culture is seen in the prism of Islam and cultural practices heavily informed by the holy book (Quran). Despite the Kings holding the chief political office, the culture and politics in Saudi Arabia not that much distant from those of a religious state where the state structures regulate the social and cultural life of society in the name of Islam and the purity of Arabism. It is an Islamic state with Wahhabi Islam as the main defining element. For example, regardless of the reasons of your travel to Saudi Arabia, it is common to see airport customs officers, paid by the state, trying to preach you about Islam and solicit your conversion to Islam (Halliday 2000:169.). Officers enforce laws that are heavily informed by Islam and searching for alcohol and other prohibited imports at the same time spreading the message of Islam to people considered non-Muslims.

However, there is one kind semi-secular national cultural holiday known as *al-Jinadiria*. On this day and event Saudis can express themselves more freely in public (Halliday 2000:169). It is celebrated with a fair of camel-racing in the day and metaphysics at night that shed light on the society and its concerns. Members of the royal family, the powerful political group in Saudi Arabia, participate in *Arada*, which includes Bedouin operetta, and tribal dance accompanied by hundreds of Saudi men who dance and enjoy their time on the stage. The sword dance is the single most vital dance in the Arabia Peninsula and national dance of the Saudi Arabia. It is usually performed by men holding up their weapons and moving slowly to the beat of the drums (Maisel and Shoup 2009:98). In Saudi Arabia women do not participate in this dance because of religious segregation laws. The state also sometimes promotes a sense of national heritage through limited recognition of the architecture and artifacts from pre Islamic times. The problem with claiming Saudi Arabia past heritage is hijacked by over-zealous Wahhabis who are strongly opposed to any facts that predate Islam (Halliday 2000:174). The concern from these ultra-conservative religious groups has in the past hindered the opening of a national archaeological museum in the country and blocked the opening of lavish cultural centers completed some years ago.

Saudi Arabia is a country that is tightly controlled, most noticeably political: no political parties or independent publications are tolerated (Halliday 2000:172). While the country follows strict Islamic rules, there are many exceptions especially with regards to the royal family. There is growing corruption and embezzlement of state funds and properties by royal families with no accountability (Halliday 2000:175). The Guardian citing WikiLeaks sources showed that whisky and other very expensive liquor are imported by members of the royal family and are served in closed social gatherings (The Guardian 2010). Many other prohibited imports are sold in underground markets throughout the country.

Women are almost entirely absent from the public space in Saudi Arabia, mostly seen covered in black veils at shopping malls and around town driven by relative male drivers or immigrant workers from Southeast Asia, Africa and, the Middle East. At universities women students have to follow lectures through videos linkups and conduct tutorials by telephone. Yet levels of education among women are high in Saudi. About 65% of graduates from Riyadh University in 1999 were women with some sectors dominated by women. However, their political and social power is crippled by the orthodox interpretation of Islam and Sharia being the law of the land (Halliday 2000:173; Long 2005:41). In Saudi Arabia, for the most part, women are still relegated to managing the household and raising children. However, with changing economic social conditions there appears to be more acceptances by men about expanding women's participation in professional careers outside of the home. There remains however, a strong male resistance to playing an active role in the household and rearing children (Long 2005:40). Polygamous marriage, in a declining trend is still common in Saudi Arabia where many wives work together in the household to support each other in house management and raising kids. Women feel traditional cultural gender roles such as denying their right to drive and move freely without the company of their spouse or close relative limits millions of women in the Kingdom their basic right to lead normal lives (Long 2005:41). These denials are not just a social issue but also an economic one. During the pre-Islamic and pre-oil boom era some of these mobility restrictions against women might not have had that much impact or been as meaningful because most the sedentary population lived in small cities, towns, and villages where the physical distance was not that great. However, in urban society where high technological and transportation advancement exists, women find themselves isolated both socially and economically. The restriction on covering in public has much less impact than restriction on mobility. While older women and very conservative young women consider those restrictions as the symbol of social modesty, many young educated women and all women of other age groups who have visited the west or other countries do not accept the restriction placed on them. Many young women in Saudi Arabia are disoriented and face immeasurable stress because of their need to enjoy the social change brought by modernization at the same time they feel guilt for abandoning their traditional Islamic social values that deny the freedom to which they aspire.

Women hold the weakest position in this patriarchal society. Women gain power within the structure by producing sons. This increases a mother's status in a family with the number of sons she bears. She can count on to even challenge his father if need be. Bonds between mothers and sons are strong, stronger than bonds between fathers and sons. In this society women do not openly challenge commands or orders but can privately appeal to reason. Their success, however, depends on whether they have sons or not (Maisel and Shoup 2009: xxx).

Saudi Arabia is governed by sharia law, which means it does not train secular lawyers. The religious judges are produced by Islamic universities and institutions (Halliday 2000:173). There is an obsessive control of every aspect of social life in Saudi Arabia that destroys the cultural diversity and oppresses the cultural values of immigrants. Freedom of speech is in many ways controlled have a laundry list of what they cannot do and which institutions are enforced in the name of public morality. Required to promote Islamic, Arabic and the Saudi kings, they ignore the larger every day experience of immigrants and women who are denied their basic freedoms. Saudi Arabia poetry, art, and literature are restricted to praise of the ruling family and their great work, with the one exception of the inspirational work of an exiled novelist Abd al-Rahman Munif. His novel, *Pillars of Sand*, portrays the corruption of dynastic rule in modern Saudi Arabia (Halidays 2000:174).

CHAPTER 6. THE VACATION, ORANGE CITY, AND NATSNET'S "GREAT ESCAPE"

Natsnet Escapes

In the early 2000's, Natsnet's Saudi Arabian family planned a vacation to the United States. Natsnet, of course, was to accompany with them. In her deposition she says, "[f]inally God heard my prayers and saw my suffering and brought me to the United States." However, her male master still needed his wife, and her domestic servant. In a luxurious American hotel, Natsnet's beating and abuse continued, but this time around was to be the last! Here, Natsnet's life changed forever.

Natsnet did not know the name of the hotel where they were staying; her masters simply had not told her. For them, Natsnet was not significant enough to be informed about such matters since she was like their luggage or other personal property without a mind, heart, or soul. She was chattel as far as they were concerned, she says.

After their arrival in Orange City, Natsnet started to look at things very carefully. She was thinking of a possible escape, but it would take a monumental act of will to do so. She played the game of docility and obedience, making sure that the Saudi Arabian couple had not the slightest hint of her thoughts. She was the ever-obedient servant, convincing them of her loyalty, but waiting for her opportunity.

The trip was planned for 60 days. On the fourth day, the wife gruffly, as usual, told her to iron their clothes. Natsnet began to iron, but the wife was not pleased. She wanted Natsnet to do things more quickly. Natsnet was just not fast enough; of course, she was never as fast as the wife wanted. The Saudi woman slapped her on her face and hit her on her side. Not only was this the straw that broke Natsnet's back, an act of torture in America, the land that Natsnet had heard was free but it was Natsnet's chance. Her will to live a normal life was unleashed and, in that instant, she decided to make her escape. If her attempt failed, it could not be worse than the life she had been living for years with her masters.

Her escape was ingeniously simple. When her masters were distracted, she just left the hotel and walked away, knowing only that she was in the fabled America, of which she had only the vaguest knowledge, and perhaps in a place called Orange City, of which she knew nothing. Natsnet recalls walking and walking the streets of the strange city not knowing where she really was or where she was going. She moved along a crowded six-lane highway really one of Orange City's major thoroughfares and was frightened by the mass of traffic, nearly overcome by the smell of exhaust, and deafened by the noise of the semis. This America was scary! Is this what freedom means?

Natsnet did not know to whom she could talk and from whom she could seek help. She could not have spoken English even if she had wanted to and she did not know the culture of this strange, new society except that it was America and Americans were supposed to be good people. She was just happy to be out of her masters' hands, but was unsure what the future held.

Ayou and Tesfaye

Natsnet says that she prayed to God to guide her, to lead her to someone who could help her. Like a dream come true, she saw a *Habesha*[1] woman coming out of a supermarket. The woman carried herself with a sense of grace typical of Horn of African women, her slender body and bronzed features sharply defined like so many of the people with whom Natsnet had been raised.

Natsnet ran to the lady and literally hugged and kissed the woman while crying uncontrollably. A surprised Ethiopian lady was not sure what was going on, but she tried to soothe Natsnet. After a few minutes, Natsnet told the lady her situation, still crying, but now these were tears of relief and joy.

Very saddened by the situation, the Ethiopian lady also started to shed tears and comforted Natsnet. There, on a street corner outside a supermarket in Orange City, the two women embraced tenderly, comforting each other. Natsnet had just experienced her first gift of kindness in a strange new country that was to become her home.

The Ethiopian woman, Ayou, took Natsnet to her home where she and Tesfaye, her husband, invited Natsnet to stay for as long as she needed. This act of kindness and gracious generosity to strangers is characteristic of the cultures of the Horn of Africa and now Natsnet found it and was experiencing it in Orange City. This was the beginning of a new chapter in Natsnet's life that was filled with the ups and downs, joys and frustrations, of the daily life of an immigrant in a new country.

In Natsnet's own words, she felt that this was the work of God, who saw her suffering and listened to her prayers.

> In Saudi Arabia, I was always praying to my God for the day to come when He would get me out of those conditions. God listened to my prayers and heard my prayers. He saw my suffering and brought me to the United States. The family, my "masters," came to the US for a visit and I was brought along to take care of their kids and do servant's chores. I thanked my God for being with me all the time and bringing me to this land of freedom.

Natsnet's First Months in America:

During her stay in the Ethiopian couple's house Natsnet enjoyed all the cultural practices and the delicious food she has been missing for years. Every weekend, Natsnet accompanied the Ethiopian couple to St. Mena's, one local center of Coptic Orthodox worship. Going to church was a dream come true for Natsnet, who had not been to church since her arrival in Saudi Arabia. Unlike this new country, America, in Saudi Arabia, with its oppressive political system and disdain for immigrants, she had been absolutely denied the right to practice her religion. Now she could do so once again.

Natsnet found joy in the Divine Liturgy. It provided her with much needed spiritual energy to connect with God in a spiritual venue. The liturgy, the singing and intonations, even the drums on the high holidays all of this reminded her of the Medhane Alem congregation in Asmara that she so regularly attended and loved so much. The church in Orange City was full of arts of the iconic representations of the saints, Gospel personages, and apostles that are unique to the Orthodox Church and reminiscent of the arts that she grew up seeing and admiring in Orthodox churches in Eritrea. Natsnet says she was especially attracted to a wall picture hanging on the Gospel side of the church portraying the Blessed Virgin Mary and her beloved son, Jesus Christ.

> When I saw the Saint Mary and Jesus Christ picture hanging on the wall, I could see my Dad and Mom with my brothers and sisters just standing below it and closing their eyes in prayer praising the Lord. It touched me so much and my eyes were full of tears and reminded me of the good days back home that I spent with my family, especially, the Easter celebration at the Medhane Alem church in Asmara.

After church Natsnet enjoyed the coffee ceremony in Ayou and Tesfaye's home and her new *Habesha* friends. They would sit, chatting for hours, telling of their memories and their past lives "back home." This was a theme that united them just as it unites newcomers in new lands all over the world.

The coffee ceremony is a typical *Habesha* cultural practice, done in Ethiopia and Eritrea, generally on weekends or holidays. Families make coffee and drink it for more than three hours. The ritual begins with the "celebrant" always a woman sitting on a small three-legged stool, roasting the coffee beans in a small pan on a hot plate placed in front of her. Once the roasting is done, the coffee maker goes around the group waving the coffee smoke towards the guests. In turn, the guests smell it, comment on its fragrance. It is part of the tradition for each guest to say *betam tiru now* (Amharic*) or Tu'um Bun* (Tigrinya) which means (lovely!) or "great coffee" or "wonderfully done" or others of phrases of praise. After this, the beans are ground with a mortar and pestle and poured into a special pot for brewing. This social event, meant to unite family, friends, and a people in a celebratory atmosphere, is a *Habesha* cultural practice performed wherever *Habesha* live.

When the coffee is done brewing, it is dark and strong and is poured into small china cups with a large amount of sugar. The cups themselves are kept in a special case. Over the course of the ceremony, at least three cups are accepted by each guest and slowly sipped with the third cup bringing a blessing to the drinker. Each delicate china cup is usually embossed with the national flag of the host family, emblematic of the integral role of family, community, religion, and culture in Ethiopian and Eritrean societies and part of a larger cultural construct in which traditional ceremonies are a part of nation and statehood. Sometime an aromatic leavened bread, popcorn, or cracker like cakes made of toasted wheat, are served with the coffee and passed from guest to guest.

The implements used in the coffee ceremony are an important part of the family's possessions and are carefully washed and securely put away after each use.

Natsnet loved making and serving the coffee and usually volunteered to host the après-church coffee ceremony at Tesfaye and Ayou's house. During the coffee ceremony, it is customary to tease someone for a real or imagined foible or recently made gaffe. One day Natsnet made a joke when everybody failed to say "Great coffee" or any praise phrases, exaggerated or not. She told everyone who had come to the ceremony, "[t]oday I am breaking this coffee pot and buying another one, because the only reason the coffee is not good is not because of me but it is because of the coffee pot." It was a polite or humorous way of telling people that lavish and exaggerated expressions of thanks after the ceremony are appropriate and part of the entire ceremony itself. When people heard Natsnet's joke they broke into laughter and everybody stood up and apologized for not saying *Tu'um Bun* (delicious coffee) or *betam tiru now.*

However, Natsnet was making a political statement about her past life in Saudi Arabia as well, by implicitly blaming someone else for her own mistakes. In this case she was blaming the coffee pot for the bad taste, which is similar to the Saudi Arabian family's placing on her all the blame for the things that went wrong in the family household. Blaming the victim was the norm in Saudi Arabia and Natsnet was always on the receiving end in a system where might made right. However, poking fun at her hard life, and her new social platform afforded by the Ethiopian family, gave Natsnet the opportunity to make friends and to get to know people.

Those who do not understand *Habesha* culture might think Eritreans and Ethiopians do not get along. After all, the Eritrean state, and much of its communal sense of statehood, was spawned and nurtured by the war of liberation from Ethiopia. The 1998 to 2000 border war was a vicious struggle and the causalities on both sides were high. However, the two peoples have shown fraternity and collaboration in every corner of the world. The hospitality and care Natsnet received from the Ethiopian couple was only one example of thousands of good deeds that exemplify the two peoples, both at home and abroad. Despite the fighting between their governments, Eritreans and Ethiopians in the diaspora continue to work and live together, and help each other in times of need. After all, they are the same people who have lived for years together and shared the same culture, history, and circumstances for centuries.

The *Habesha* community embraced her and provided her with financial and moral support after her escape. They consoled her and worked tirelessly to heal the physical and mental wounds she suffered at the hands of the oppressive Saudi Arabian family. Many of her Ethiopian and Eritrean friends started to help her and many were very kind.

This much-needed social support and counseling made Natsnet's life in the Orange City a lot better, and encouraged her to work hard to assimilate into American life, striving like all immigrants to achieve the American dream, while maintaining her own cultural integrity. By this, Natsnet did not mean giving up her own heritage by disappearing into an amorphous melting pot or even stew pot. Rather, she strove to become part of a larger salad bowl in which her own cultural dignity was maintained while uniting with others in a liberal multicultural social order.

Natsnet Strikes Out on Her Own:

After nearly a year living with Tesfaye and Ayou, Natsnet felt confident to try living on her own. She was able, with their help and that of several of her friends, to rent a small studio apartment on a block in downtown Orange City where several *Habesha* families lived. She became part of the nascent Eritrean-Ethiopian community in Orange City.

In mid-2000, with the help of an attorney, Natsnet began the application process for political asylum. This was the beginning of a long struggle to stay in America legally. When it was legally permissible, she obtained a work permit and started to work as a waitress in a Mexican restaurant. She spoke a bit of Spanish because of its similarity to Italian and this helped. She began to share and enjoy the freedom people have in this country. Those days were the most enjoyable times in her life. There was no one who hit her, beat her, insulted her, or hurt her. She became the owner of herself, and began to lead her own life. "I thank God from the bottom of my heart for the opportunity and freedom I thought would never come," she says.

While working at the restaurant, she met an Eritrean guy. They started dating and were talking of a wedding and family. Natsnet soon produced a daughter named Tesfa, who is now in her late childhood and a son Daniel in his early childhood. Natsnet and her ex-boyfriend had a good three years. Life seemed to move very smoothly but as the months passed, her ex-boyfriend and Natsnet's notions of responsibility and thrift started to differ radically. Quarrelling between the two began. After a few years, their relationship ended and Natsnet was heartbroken. Her dream of having a traditional Eritrean family and married life like that of her parents, only here in America, slipped away from her.

Her breakup with her ex-boyfriend was culturally devastating since Natsnet had grown up in a very traditional Christian family where the sanctity of marriage and family is highly respected. It was very hard to tell her parents in Eritrea that her relationship with the man whom she expected to become her husband was now over. In the culture in which she had grown up, the bearing of children out of wedlock had negative connotations, even shame attached to them. She felt betrayed by a man whom she had trusted, with whom she shared happy moments, and together had made a beautiful daughter and son.

Once again, the Eritrean and Ethiopian community in Orange City stood behind her and promised to work with her and her ex to try to reconcile their differences and get the two of them back together. However, like Humpty Dumpty, things could not be put back together, and Natsnet's fight to survive and support her children and herself continued. Now looming over her was Natsnet's continued inability to communicate and understand the nuanced cultural system of the United States. This inability caused Natsnet problem after problem.

Even before her relationship failed, things had begun to go badly for Natsnet with the denial of her asylum application. Her application fell apart in March of that year, when her petition was denied and her application to renew her work permit was also denied. Natsnet explains as follows:

> I saw two attorneys, but my memory of those days is not clear. Things all run together. I remember that I just did not communicate well with either. Neither attorney really understood my case and I just did not know what was happening. I could not understand. It was just so complicated! I only speak a little English and there was just a complete misunderstanding between both lawyers and me.

Natsnet remembers seeing her first lawyer only twice, both in court hearings. She spoke to her on the phone only twice, both times very briefly. She seemed like a nice lady to her. Natsnet does not know and no one knows what would have happened had she not passed away sometime in mid-2000s. Natsnet then saw a second attorney with whom she spoke only four times, each time for about ten minutes. She really can't remember the details of what happened with either the first or second attorney.

She had trusted the people around her because of the skill she mistakenly thought they had in immigration matters and her attorneys whom she assumed to be competent with the preparation of her documents, especially her deposition. Natsnet only vaguely knew what a deposition was let alone the material it should contain. The latter document was critical since its purpose was to tell her story and make her plea for asylum.

Her second attorney included a statement in the deposition that Natsnet was not aware of. She wrote that Natsnet was an Erob, an ethnic group that lives in southern Eritrea near her parents' village. Many people in Eritrea do not think of Erobs as Eritreans and there is discrimination and government mistreatment of them. In truth, Natsnet was not Erob. She was simply unaware that the attorney had written this, and she naively signed the deposition, trusting in the attorney's competence and her friends' advice.

The result was a deposition absolutely lacking in substance, prepared without adequate competent advice, nearly devoid of reality. Natsnet recalls, "The presiding judge, was absolutely astounded with the inconsistencies and poor preparation of the case". The judge asked her about Erobs/Irobs[2] and she frankly told her that she had no idea about what she was being asked. She was not Erob, period! She had hardly consulted with her lawyer on the deposition and the person who was helping her was not as knowledgeable as she had thought. In her asylum hearing, the respected judge had no option other than to deny her asylum application.

After that, Natsnet's life went downhill. Since her work permit was denied, she couldn't work. She was unable to provide for Tesfa and Daniel as she would have liked. She often relied on the generosity of her small but loyal group of friends to help with necessities as well as rent. Tesfaye and Ayou had moved to the suburbs of Orange City when Tesfaye got a promotion that put him on the road a lot. As a result, her contact with them slowly ended.

Natsnet was so stressed and depressed: it seemed that the freedom and opportunity God had given to her was just slipping away, piece by piece, bit by bit. She found herself spending her days praying to God to give her the freedom and opportunity that he gave to all Americans.

Natsnet was facing grave issues in her personal life and fighting to secure her freedom through the immigration system. However, she was also learning about American culture and customs making all kinds of observations in her new life in America. The differences between life here in the United States and Natsnet's experiences in Saudi Arabia a country that Natsnet had internalized as "normal" from her perspective there as a domestic worker were stark and startling. This was especially true for American women whose behavior and fashion choices would have shocked her only a few years before: immodest styles of dress; tight jeans and shorts; swim suits; walking alone; couples engaging in public displays of affection kissing in public; vigorous political expression and political discourse. All of these was draped in what seemed to be a façade of equality and public respect. Was all of this real, Natsnet asked herself.

For Natsnet, America was totally unchartered territory, a *tabla rosa,* consisting of layered physical and social space mixed with individual freedom and genial faces that disguised real emotions. Natsnet was "born again" as a woman who has seen so much oppression and abuse in a society where women are considered chattel. If she could not stay in America, what would happen to her? This was a concern on which Natsnet dwelt.

Natsnet Learns about US Citizenship: Despite her difficulty communicating, she was learning. Natsnet was curious about America's social and cultural values including religion, marriage and family, politics, immigration, and race and ethnicity. Its notion of citizenship intrigued her the most. Natsnet's view of citizenship was shaped by the definition of a closed Saudi Arabia and other Gulf states, not much different from her Eritrean homeland. Natsnet had begun to think of citizenship as based on ancestry, race and ethnicity, and religious affiliation. It was a closed thing into which one was born. One did not acquire it. America's concept of citizenship was grounded in a much different set of norms as an open and sometimes welcoming society which at least in theory all could join.

One example that had taken place just after Ayou and Tesfaye had taken her in is telling. Once, Natsnet referred to the couple's children as "Ethiopians." The children heard her and promptly corrected her, saying "[w]e are Americans; our parents are from Ethiopia." Natsnet did not take their view very seriously, thinking these are just kids who do not know what "citizenship" means. In the evening when Natsnet and her hosts were having dinner, she brought up the discussion. To her surprise, the parents said, '[y]es, of course, they are Americans, they were born here." The children, at least in their psyches, had internalized that citizenship went with place of birth.

These were new ideas for Natsnet and she pursued it further. The children's parents tried to explain to Natsnet by telling her that she could acquire citizenship just as they, Ayou and Tesfaye, had done several years before. There were two ways to be a citizen. You could be born here, or be born of American parents, and be regarded as a citizen. Or you could choose and undertake the naturalization process. Once you applied, had lived here for a certain number of years, passed a test, and met certain other criteria, American citizenship could be conferred.

Tesfaye and Ayou then showed Natsnet the two small American flags that they had been given at the ceremony granting them citizenship, and told Natsnet of that day. They had to travel to a distant city where there was a federal district court. The ceremony took place in an ornate courtroom, and they were sworn in by a distinguished judge of a federal Court of Appeals. There were about 100 people naturalized that day, coming from 43 countries! Ayou and Tesfaye joined one other Ethiopian in the ceremony, an older lady named Tensus. Tesfaye told Natsnet that he had cried when the national anthem was sung. Natsnet nodded her head with surprise, and smiling, she said, using one of her first pieces of American slang, "Awesome! Then I can be an American too!"

Her thoughts quickly reverted to Saudi Arabia and she said:

> You know, in Saudi Arabia it is impossible for an immigrant to get citizenship and their Saudi-born children, no matter how "Saudi" they become or how long they have been in Saudi Arabia, they can never become citizens.

She raised up her hands and said:

> Oh, America is such a great and blessed country, and I am so happy to be here. I hope God will keep my dream alive and my kids and grandkids will be proud Americans for generations to come!

At that point, Natsnet's view of things had begun to change. She was out of a country of "no" and the "impossible," and in one of "yes" and "possible," a country of so much opportunity including the ultimate prize, citizenship.

Natsnet Grows: When she came to stay in the Ethiopian couple's house, Natsnet spent her time watching television. While not understanding the discussion, she could understand the general topic of discussion. It was amazing for Natsnet to see individual citizens openly criticizing their leaders, even mocking them. Some cartoons of American politicians could be downright wicked, even from Natsnet's vantage point. This was totally surprising for Natsnet who grew up under dictatorial regimes in Asmara and did her time in Saudi Arabia, systems that deny a person their right to fulfill their potential to become a productive member of society and to pursue life as each sees fit. This was the beginning of Natsnet's introduction to democracy and the social and the political processes that come with it her process of political socialization. This was a totally new and absolutely gratifying moment that she had never experienced previously. She felt so sorry for the people she had left behind in Saudi Arabia and Eritrea, for their inability to experience the things that people enjoy in America.

Natsnet was also curious about Americans' concept of family, marriage, and romantic relationships: how people formed families. Her homeland, Eritrea, and the "land of her captivity," Saudi Arabia, share similarly strict perspectives in their views about marriage and the importance of the extended family (Torstrick and Faier 2009:110). This is the case even though Saudi Arabia is Islamic and Eritrea, Christian and Islamic. In Saudi Arabia marriage is governed by *sharia* law that defines the relationship between a man and a woman or women. In most cases marriage is arranged and could happen between cousins or other close relatives. The concept of family goes beyond the nuclear family and can include extended relatives who live in close proximity to one another. In Saudi Arabia, the concept of "boyfriend and girlfriend," or a dating relationship, does not exist and the mingling of genders, except under the most closely defined circumstances, is greatly constricted.

In Eritrea things have changed greatly in the last two decades. The number of arranged marriages has substantially declined (Gebremedhin 2001: 45-49). Among Eritrean Muslims, however, there is still marriage between cousins and close relatives. Similarly, Western-style relationships, such as couples dating, have become common. What is similar between Saudi Arabia and Eritrea is the concept of family that goes far beyond the nuclear family.

On issues that we know in the West as LGBT (i.e., lesbian, gay, bisexual, transgender), both government and society take a conservative, forbidding stance (Torstrick and Faier 2009:113). The most perplexing for Natsnet was her introduction to gay relationships. Once, in the mall, she saw two men holding hands. In a park, Natsnet saw two guys and two girls holding hands and then tightly embracing each other. At this point in her thinking, Natsnet had not yet processed the concept of gay relationships. She thought the people were holding hands because they were close friends. In Eritrea, two men who were friends, or two women, often held hands so this was a common sight in the streets of Asmara. Generally, in the culture of the Horn of Africa, this is the sign of personal affection and not of a homosexual relationship. It is merely part of the culture. However, when the two men kissed each other, she was genuinely confused.

After one of these instances, a rather blatant display of affection between two men, she called her friend Aster on her cell to tell her about what she had seen. Aster began laughing, and Natsnet asked her why, crying out excitedly, "Why are you laughing, what is this, I have not seen anything like this in my entire life." Aster told her not to worry, explaining, "They are probably just gay." Aster invited Natsnet to come to her house for a glass of wine and said, "we will talk more about it and I will explain to you over a drink when we see each other." Once she got to Aster's house and the two women started to talk, Aster explained that relationships like this are legal here and people have the right to love whomever they want.

Even though Natsnet was a very religious person and had a different moral perspective about gay relationships, she was very amazed by the degree of freedom and liberty America has to offer. She told her friend, "You see, if these guys were to do that in public in Saudi, they would be killed." Natsnet continued, "America is great and it is a country where everybody is tolerated and has the freedom to live wherever someone wants, to love whomever they want, and to practice whatever religion they wish. They can do this, but no one can force me to like it either!" Natsnet was getting it and slowly learning America's social and political fabric deeply rooted in freedom and individual liberty.

Natsnet had come a long way, not just escaping from the hands of the oppressive Saudi Arabian family, but also experiencing a land that she never thought she would see. She saw not only the shining sun of Orange City, but she also saw the shining side of American democracy. However, Natsnet also saw the bad side of America, the divide between the poor and the rich, the documented and the undocumented, the medically insured and the uninsured. The social and economic inequality was something Natsnet understood as unacceptable. The greatest of all great nations was failing to address issues of social, economic, and health inequality.

Moreover, Natsnet noticed Americans' lack of understanding of people beyond their borders. When she told others that she was from Eritrea, the answer was an inevitable "Where is that? How do you spell it?" Astoundingly to Natsnet, most Americans had only the vaguest notion of the African continent; its location, its peoples, its languages, and its cultures. She felt that something was gravely missing in the American educational system that made it hard for Americas to understand "the other." She said,

"I was taught about the rest of the world when I was in the fifth grade. How is it that a nation with so many resources fails to teach its citizens about the geography and cultures of other peoples who respect America so much and emulate Americans in so many ways?"

Notes

1. Term used to refer to people from Eritrean and Ethiopian highlands. However, the term could apply to any Ethiopian and Eritrean descent in the diaspora. Usually, is more often in the diaspora because of it neutralizes national and religious politics that exists in their home countries (Eritrean and Ethiopian).
2. They are a member of the Saho Ethnic group who live in the Mountain regions of Northeastern Ethiopia and Southeastern Eritrea. They are predominantly agriculturalist and Orthodox Christians. The Erobs/Irobs inhabited some of the contested border areas between Eritrean and Ethiopia and they were affected very much by the Ethio-Eritrean border war of 1997-2000.

CHAPTER 7. YEARS OF DOUBT, DISAPPOINTMENT, & DISILLUSIONMENT

Natsnet's Life at a Crossroads

Natsnet's fight for freedom continued with a disappointing result in her asylum application and a frustrating personal life in Orange City: asylum denied and ex-boyfriend constant maneuverings to lure Tesfa and Daniel away. Natsnet was now at a crossroads in her life, and time was running out with deportation hanging over her head. All legal avenues to remain in the United States had almost disappeared, and immigration officials were poised to forcefully deport her to a country where she would face torture, indefinite imprisonment, or even death.

Previous mismanagement of the asylum process by her lawyers was now about to cost Natsnet the freedom and protection many thought she deserved. The hopes and dreams she had for a new life in the United States were about to be dashed. Natsnet did not know much about the system, in which she was dealing, nor the professional culture and reasoning processes of her lawyers. Neither did she possess the level of knowledge, technical ability, or skills to assist actively in developing her case for asylum. Her lack of facility in English gave her no control over the stories her lawyers wrote to embellish her case. She often felt as if she was vainly crying for help, but there was no one to help her. Her reality the only thing she knew was the denial of her asylum application and orders to leave the country. She could not understand why on earth a country that cared so much about freedom and liberty would throw her into the proverbial crocodile's mouth. This interval in Natsnet's life was an absolute nightmare. It seemed that only a miracle could save her and her growing daughter and son, and let them live together in peace in America.

We have already seen the encounters Natsnet had with her two previous lawyers and the bogus deposition the second one prepared. All the effort, psychic energy, and money that Natsnet had spent, and her cries and prayers to God, had not produced a single meaningful result. Natsnet, however, did not sit idly by awaiting her fate. She actively approached others and sought their counsel and help, not their pity or charity.

Like many diasporic communities, and despite their internal differences and deep cleavages, Eritreans in America have an active and effective communications network: stories travel quickly by social networks, e-mail, and phone a modern update of "the bush telegraph." It was at this point that Irv and Dawit entered Natsnet's life, first as sympathetic listeners, then as worker companions in her struggle for asylum.

Enter Dawit and Irv

Dawit had heard of Natsnet's plight from his friend Ayana, who lived near Orange City. Dawit was born in Eritrea and is a bit younger than Natsnet; he had seen the realities of revolution in his Eritrean homeland and the grueling process of independence. He had witnessed internecine battles between Eritrean liberation forces, had experienced front-line war action, and endured his own imprisonment and torture while still in Eritrea. He told Irv, his friend in Utah, a Ph.D. in political science who saw anthropology's array of theoretical perspectives and analytic techniques as an excellent means to examine and understand political processes and behavior.

Dawit and Irv had known each other for many years. Both were interested in the Horn of Africa, its development, and its social and cultural systems. Both prized human rights. Dawit is a reformer who continues to fight and advocate for an independent and democratic Eritrea; Irv had worked for most of his professional career in the American civil rights struggle. Both were deeply touched by Natsnet's story and realized that Natsnet would be consigned by the immigration system to an unending hell if she did not receive professional help and she needed it quickly. They both thought that the asylum process could be made to work if a "player" had the skills, patience, and resources to make it work. If Natsnet could not do this on her own, then Irv and Dawit could at least help. It was their task, their personal and professional obligation, to assist her to make the system work for her and not against her. However, before anything could begin, Dawit and Irv had to raise the needed funds to cover the legal costs. With the help of Natsnet's congregation and her friends, Irv and Dawit raised the necessary money.

In the initial stages, Dawit's priority was to console and reassure Natsnet who was near her psychological breaking point. His reassuring Tigrinya words were a great comfort to Natsnet. The next step was finding an attorney to handle her case. Dawit and Irv did a yellow-pages, and internet search and came up with a law firm specializing in immigration law and asylum matters. The firm was located in a town not that far from Orange City. The firm proprietor is a well-respected attorney who had some familiarity with the African continent and hired a new attorney to work on different immigration cases. There was more than one attorney involved in Natsent case. We will refer them as the "Legal team" as we narrate our interaction with them in working with Natsent's case.

A Microcosm of the Immigration Attorney's World: One of the attorneys (the lead attorney) assigned to Natsnet's case, was a young hotshot from a highly regarded law school in the US. He/she had exceptional background in immigration law, especially asylum law, and lots of in-court experience. Along the way, he/she had gathered plaudits from his/her legal comrades and awards from professional organizations. She/he seemed the perfect match for Natsnet.

Together, Irv and Dawit made a good team functioning as Natsnet's mediators in relating to newly hired attorney. Dawit was the cultural interlocutor, translator, comforter, and much more. As the first-language-English speaker, Irv main work was to make sure Natsnet ideas and thought are correctly translated into western legal language. As things developed, his first task was to work with Dawit in preparing Natsnet's deposition. Then, his specific ongoing job was to put together "expert testimony" supporting Natsnet's petition to reopen her asylum proceedings. His work described the social and political conditions in Eritrea and what would probably happen to Natsnet if she were sent back to her homeland.

BACKGROUND SECTION NO. 4:

From Irv's Deposition: What Would Happen to Natsnet if She Were Deported to Eritrea

God forbid, should the Respondent be returned to Eritrea, in my judgment this is a probable scenario. She would:

a. Arrive at Asmara International Airport in the company of a US Government-sanctioned escort;
b. Be immediately segregated from the other passengers on the aircraft, escorted off, and taken to a special section of the airport where she would be interrogated, subject to verbal abuse, arrested; and
c. Be taken to a local detention facility where she would face more questioning, verbal harassment, and even physical abuse.

She would then be transferred to a permanent place of imprisonment, perhaps as with so many others in similar situations, in the western part of the country, one of the hottest geographic locations on earth. Her cell might consist of a shipping container, crowded with others, unbearably hot in daytime and harshly cold at night.

The interrogation would be unending, the verbal harassment and psychological terror nearly unbearable, and the physical abuse intensified. The Respondent would weaken under all of this physical and psychological strain, perhaps become seriously ill, and decline. She could even be killed.

Her parents who were eagerly waiting to greet their beloved daughter after an absence of over 10 years, upon her arrival at Asmara international Airport would be detained and warned of pursuing their daughter. Other threats would be made against them and they would be made aware of the Eritrean State's control over them and their affairs. They would be reminded of what had happened to their liquor store business (It was closed because of her and her brother escape from the government control) and of the power of the Eritrean state. It would be emphasized to them that their daughter was a practitioner of a banned faith and all of her other acts defying the State. It is possible that they would be jailed for a day or two, before finally being released and placed under surveillance.

The Respondent would experience all of the noxiousness and malignity of the Eritrean prison system documented in this deposition, in the works cited by it, and by my previous deposition.

To conclude, should Respondent be returned to Eritrea, she faces at best a life of prison, harassment, and horrors or at worse death.

Their initial faith in the attorney was diminished somewhat when he/she asked them, in all seriousness, to tell her/him the dominant religion of Saudi Arabia. In other instances, the attorney demonstrated a profound lack of geopolitical knowledge. Cultural differences and nuances eluded this particular attorney. The attorney's world of reasoning, like many others in the legal and medical world, was very limited. The attorney's sense of "how things were" was steeped in western legal cultural concepts into which he/she had been socialized by law school, and reinforced daily by her/his professional culture and work environment. He/she was imprisoned by that culture, unable to break free of it.

Regarding the attorneys' geopolitical knowledge, Dawit and Irv wrote in an internal memorandum that reminded the attorneys about the cultural, political and social dynamics that have to be looked at differently. Dawit and Irv constantly asked the attorneys to have an alternative perspective from the western mindset and to examine the situation within the local context.

In another instance, Natsnet's brother, Yohannes, and his flight from Eritrea (escaping the religious harassment he suffered in National Service) through Sudan and Libya to Europe, became relevant to Natsnet's case. The attorney was puzzled, asking why Yohannes had not sought asylum in one of the African countries (Libya) through which he had passed. The reality of these countries' political orientations, and their hostile feelings towards Eritrean refugees or the political condition of these countries, had simply escaped the attorneys.

Dawit and Irv, however, had to play on the legal teams' turf, and they quickly learned to think "legalese," translating real world ideas into categories and concepts that fit within a legal worldview. Their one on one encounters with American immigration attorneys with their ecclesiastical system of reasoning and generally limited view of the geopolitics constituted another landmark on the journey Natsnet was traveling.

At each stage of the process, beginning with the relationship between the petitioner and the attorney, the powerlessness and near insignificance of the petitioner is emphasized, and the dominance of "the other" highlighted. Dawit and Irv with their respective personal, academic, and vocational backgrounds were able to equalize, if only a bit, Natsnet's relative position, at least in her relationship with the attorneys. The attorneys at times felt their hegemonic position in the case has been challenged because of this new arrangement. Dawit and Irv however, worked patiently with the team, gaining insights into their thinking and behavior along the way. Their first substantive legal task was to work with Natsnet in preparing her deposition, telling her story, and laying the base for the further development of her case that would come in the following months and years.

The authors understand they are here using relatively strong languages that were used throughout the legal process but they want to provide the readers with the tension, frustration, and at times hopelessness that could be caused because of the communication and knowledge gap that existed between the legal team and the client team. Not only on this case, both of the authors worked with lawyers and attorneys for years on Eritrean and Ethiopian immigration cases. This is a systematic observation they have made over the years. They strongly feel this is a systemic failure in the legal training with regards to cultural competence and geopolitical understanding. These are very good people and very committed to their work and their profession but are trained to think in certain ways that hamper their ability to deal with the diverse cultural reasoning and backgrounds of their clients.

The First Legal Test: the legal team's first legal test was to get Natsnet's asylum case reopened, thus giving Natsnet another shot to appeal for asylum. By reopening the case, the court would lift the deportation order hanging over her. In order to do this, Natsnet or those doing her case had to show that conditions in Eritrea had substantially changed since the time of her original petition was filed, and that she was fearful of persecution because of her membership or association with one or more of five protected classes: race, religion, nationality, political opinion, or social group. Religious persecution and overall persistent human right deterioration in Eritrea were the opening to get the asylum case reopened.

For most of her life, Natsnet had been a member of the Medhane Alem Movement within the Eritrean Orthodox Church. Medhane Alem has been described as a Sunday school movement, generally a reformist strain with alleged Pentecostal bent, within the Eritrean Church. It has deep roots and a long history in the world of Coptic Christianity. When Natsnet left Eritrea for Saudi Arabia in mid-1990s, the Medhane Alem Movement under the umbrella of the Eritrean Orthodox Church was a government-recognized religious organization and free to practice. In the mid-2000s, the government turned on the movement, seeing it as a challenge to state power. It was essentially banned, its places of worship raided by government security personnel, and its leadership and many of its members, particularly those who were outspoken, jailed. This was the key "changed country conditions" to getting the deportation order lifted and Natsnet's plea for asylum heard again.

BACKGROUND SECTION NO. 5:

The Medhane Alem Movement within the Eritrean Orthodox Church

When in Eritrea, Natsnet was an active member of the Eritrean Orthodox Medhane Alem congregation in Asmara, which is similar to the largest rock-hewn church in Lalibela, Ethiopia, constructed in the 12th or 13th century, and a symbol of Orthodoxy's antiquity in the Horn of Africa. (For reference purposes, the Eritrean Orthodox Church is sometimes called the Coptic Orthodox Church.) Natsnet's parish is the center of a renewal movement within the Orthodox Church known by the parish's name, the Medhane Alem movement. Her family members were all devout adherents of the Orthodox Church and are still practicing Orthodox Christians. Her brothers and other members of her extended family are also practicing members of Medhane Alem Church.

The Medhane Alem movement within the Eritrean Orthodox Church represents, in large measure, a response to the emergence of fundamentalist Protestant congregations in Eritrea (e.g., assemblies of Jehovah's Witnesses, Pentecostal groups, etc.) and the robust proselytizing techniques these groups use to spread their beliefs and to gain converts. The Medhane Alem movement sees as its role model the work of Archdeacon Habeeb Guirgus of the Egyptian Coptic Church who led a renewal and revitalization movement in that church during the early part of the 20th century.

Islamist culture confronted the Egyptian church. Traditionally within the Oriental Orthodox family of churches, the Egyptian Coptic Church is viewed as *primus inter pares*. After Eritrea achieved de jure independence in 1993, the Eritrean Orthodox Church formally became independent. (Formerly, of course, the Eritrean church was a diocese of the Ethiopian Tewahdo Orthodox Church.) A protocol was signed with the Egyptian church and the Orthodox Church in Eritrea became a full-fledged member of the Oriental family of churches, just as the Ethiopian church had done in 1959. Since then, the patriarch of the Egyptian church customarily ordains the Eritrean patriarch. In Ge'ez, the liturgical language of the Eritrean and Ethiopian Orthodox Tewahdo Churches, "Medhane Alem" means "Savior of the World." The movement is also referred to as a "renewal," "reform," "revitalization," "revival," "Bible study," or "Sunday School" movement, all having parallels with Archdeacon Guirgus' work in the Egyptian church.

Many members of the Eritrean intellectual elite are attracted to the Medhane Alem movement. Like Christian movements in other parts of Africa, its teachings focus on the Bible and biblical lessons for today's world. The movement is fueled by the government's increasingly repressive stance. The Medhane Alem movement within the Eritrean Orthodox Church represents a young (in spirit or age) person's church a vibrant and synergistic mix of Orthodox belief and mysticism with contemporary Christian witness and expression.

Some in the Eritrean Orthodox Church, which has traditionally been seen as supportive of or subservient to the regime, perceive the Medhane Alem movement as a threat to the church's power. Some in the government also see the movement as a threat; Medhane Alem vigorously opposes government intervention in the affairs of the Church. In essence, the Medhane Alem movement is a semi-independent, emerging force within Eritrean society, and is perceived by some key actors, especially in the government, as a challenge to their vested interests. Entrenched authoritarian regimes, demanding the supreme loyalty of their citizens, as does the Eritrean regime, often perceive such societal forces and independent centers of power as threatening.

The government of Eritrea recognizes only four religious bodies, all with traditional roots in Eritrea. These are the Eritrean Orthodox Tewahdo Church, the Evangelical Church (Lutheran), the Roman Catholic Church, and Islam (Sunni). It has been unlawful for anyone to worship – even in private homes – under the auspices of any other denomination since May 2002. The US Department of State has documented many instances of abuse of religious freedom since 2002, especially for those adherents of non-registered religious bodies. In September 2004, the US Department of State named Eritrea as a Country of Particular Concern (CPC) under the 1998 religious Freedom Act for Eritrea's failure to address flagrant and persistent violations of religious freedom. Sanctions were imposed the following year under the Arms Export Control Act. This was reaffirmed by the Department of State each year afterwards and as recently as 2014.

Early on, Medhane Alem movement adherents, as part of the Orthodox Church, were relatively free from governmental interference in their religious activities. Since February 2004, however, the Medhane Alem movement has been viewed with increasing suspicion, distrust, and even fear by the Eritrean government. This has resulted in the harassment and detention of its adherents, including children; the excommunication of key movement members via governmental manipulation; the arrest of its priests; the closing of its places of worship; the deposition of the Orthodox patriarch (known in Ge'ez as *abune*) – in part over his defense of the Medhane Alem movement; and the installation of a government-sponsored successor. In its 2008 *World Report*, Human Rights Watch stated that "[m]embers of the renewal movement [referring to Medhane Alem] have been arrested and abused in the same fashion as members of non-recognized churches."

More Challenges with Attorneys: The case proceeded, but sometimes at a snail's pace. Communication between Natsnet, through Irv and Dawit, and the legal team continue to be very difficult. The lead legal team was an intelligent and aggressive young attorney, but he/she had a difficult time relating to his/her client. His/her "attorney-speak," lack of geopolitical competence, the clients country of origin, and cultural barriers made it a trying process just as the legal process itself was time consuming. For the next three years, this was to be Irv and Dawit's life, working with this legal team.

Quotations from internal memoranda between Dawit and Irv illustrate the point. Regarding his/her general orientation towards the world, his/her clients, and his/her job (Note: This memorandum is substantially modified to fit an academic audience and to disguise the people involved in the case) Irv and Dawit wrote:

> Dear legal team, it would be well advised to look at the case from its cultural, historical and political context instead of projecting a western worldview to it. Social reality is a product of a particular group or person's perceptions or experiences. Different groups and people structure social reality differently.
>
> While we strongly respect your work and your profession, we believe our expertise, informed from our own social science discipline (Anthropology and political science), could greatly help to fill the gap that exists between the client and your team. We see the legal teams' job as the legal interlocutors as taking the principals' stories as they are, in the voices of the storytellers, and then drawing from them the points necessary to develop his/her own legal document as a separate work product. At the same time, we could serve

> as cultural interlocutors between you and Natsnet making sure that the clients story is correctly translated into a western cultural view and meaning. The stories that stem from other cultures do not come neatly packaged in western cultural and legalistic terms. One worldview cannot be imposed on another if any degree of credibility is to be projected. Taking others' stories as they are, and treating them with respect is one thing. Then translating those stories into legal categories is another task.

As an example, let us consider the basic idea of how people call themselves: what a person's name is, how one calls him or herself, is an important and affirmatively positive identifying mark. It just matters! Understanding naming systems that follow rationales other than the Western European model (i.e., First/Personal/Christian name + Middle Name + Family Name/Surname as in Irvin Howard Bromall) is a difficult concept that many have struggled to grasp. Semitic names follow a different scheme (i.e., Personal Name + Personal Name of Father + Personal Name of Paternal Grandfather as in Dawit Okubatsion Woldu). This is the biblical notion of "son/daughter of." The legal team constantly referred to Ms. Natsnet as "Ms. T'eum." The name T'eum that appeared as her "last name" to the attorney was really her father's first name, an expression of her lineage. Natsnet was her name first and last. To address her as Ms. T'eum and not Ms. Natsnet simply missed the point. Again, in vernacular, to "mess up" a person's name is to" mess" with the person as a person. We do not blame the legal team because they were not aware of those naming difference because they were not trained to think differently about other cultures. The western naming system was the model they have used in their training and they forced those models on their clients in their professional career regardless of the clients' backgrounds. To affirm this attorney's reasoning process, we were continually making systematic observations about the inability of the attorneys to comprehend these cultural differences that had major implication in the client and attorney communication. We asked an attorney who was closely working on the case about this problem. The person's response was "We are thought to think in a western model regardless of the person's cultural and social background and in fact at times there is a lack of even recognition that there might be a cultural factor to a case interpretation or overall miscommunication. It simply is not emphasized both in the training and work environment and it is mostly left to you, the attorney, personal experience and discretion on any cultural or social factors."

Constant mishandling of her case had already traumatized Natsnet, making her suspicious of everything. The mistakes in her name, a minor cultural faux pas to some, only further unnerved her. Those present in the court could see this in her face and expression. At this point, not only was Natsnet a nonperson, essentially powerless, but she was increasingly becoming alienated from the very process that could set her free.

One rather bizarre situation complicated the situation even further. At one point, the attorney office insisted on Natsnet's taking a lie-detector test to establish her credibility. Their goal was to overcome the negative feelings regarding her believability left by the perjury charge against her: signing in total ignorance, but good faith, the document stating that she was of Erob descent. Not only were funds not available for such a test, such a procedure would have alienated Natsnet even further. Coming from Natsnet's cultural background, the thought of wiring her up to a machine, and then interrogating her, was simply not wise. At that point, Natsnet was again nearing her breaking point. Dawit and Irv objected, but tried to "interpret" the attorney's demand to Natsnet who continued to balk. The legal team and Natsnet both were persistent in their arguments.

Instead, Irv and Dawit proposed a compromise. One of Irv's professional acquaintances was a psychologist practicing psychological counseling and evaluation in Utah. Why not engage him to do a psychological evaluation of Natsnet by telephone? The legal team agreed and the evaluation was conducted. Dawit served as translator. After the interview, when Dawit summarized the call with Natsnet to Irv, he was simply stunned by the psychological trauma this woman went through. The psychologist's evaluation showed that Natsnet was deeply affected psychologically by the asylum drama she was enduring and all that she had undergone, especially in Saudi Arabia. The law office included the psychological write-up with Natsnet's case submission at the appropriate time. It seemed that all parties were happy with the compromise.

Another area of discord inhibiting open communication were the cultural differences in the reckoning of time from Natsnet's perspective and conventional western usage. Anglo Saxon legal usage places great importance on exactness in dates, precise times, and linear sequencing of events. Judges like a precisely stated time line (i.e., X → Y →Z). Finding inconsistencies in a petitioner's rendering of his/her story is a major cause for the dismissal of many asylum petitions. Any mistake in dates, often reflecting only a differing cultural understanding of time and storytelling, significantly damages the credibility of the client's case.

Natsnet herself told her story from a Semitic/Eritrean point of view, not from a western perspective. This means that rather than tying a specific event to a precise and definitive date, things are much more likely to be expressed in terms of general clusters of events, happening "around" a specific time or "seasons" or special cultural or religious events. In order to translate Natsnet's story to "West-speak," Irv and Dawit asked the lawyers to see Natsnet's storytelling along these lines. This might be subtle, but it is of critical importance that those who advocate for a petitioner understand the dynamics of the petitioner's cultural background and thought patterns. In fact in many African countries and cultures, particularly in rural areas, birthdates and other special dates, that are very important in western cultures, are not recorded. For example, in Eritrea, people do not celebrate their birthdays after three or four years old. In many cases people just do not know their birthdate and they were not officially recorded until a few years ago. In fact many people give a random or approximate birthdate when they apply for their passports when they come to the US or Europe. There is a joke within the *Habesha* community that says every *Habesha* was born during the first week of January. It is a generalizing statement to some degree but there is some truth to it. To attest that, Dawit's gets many birthday alerts in his social media account (especially on facebook) during January from his *Habesha* friends than during any other month. Therefore, time concepts are culturally constructed and would not be a useful means to investigate in asylum hearings whether a person is a "liar" or "genuine" at least for this specific social group.

In a private conversation with Dawit, Natsnet revealed her concern about one of the lawyers in the law office. She said:

> These people might be smart and very good at their work, but I am having a hard time relating to them. One of them speaks so fast and doesn't listen to others. I am just worried

> at this moment! They need to listen to my concerns and really need to get what I feel and to the problems I am facing, both personally and legally. You know!

Natsnet begins to cry, continuing in a rumpling voice that has seen so much pain, frustration, and fear.

> Somebody has to listen and pay attention to what I am saying. I do not need someone to scare me with a high-pitched voice in my ear with some pessimistic statements. I need someone to empower me and encourage me by saying, "do not worry!" Talk to me in a soft voice and ask me questions that are really relevant to the case. I do not think these people have that ability, or even understand how they come off to me I am deeply concerned.

Natsnet's legal team, as well as other immigration attorneys but certainly not all displayed an abysmal lack of cultural competence in their understanding of different culturally related patterns of naming, time recognition, and the geography and the sociopolitical context in which clients' cases are grounded. Both Irv and Ḍawit felt that in arguing Natsnet's case, and in interacting with Natsnet, elements of cultural and political relevance should be considered and addressed.

Sometimes the communication between the attorneys and Irv and Dawit was tense because of disagreements on the operational style of both the deposition and the expert witness document. Major modification to expertise witness document and taking out some key ideas from deposition were major contended areas including the tendency to use sensationalism in those documents such as the use of "sex slave" that projects some negative image of people. At times Dawit and Irv also felt a degree of disrespect, lack of email response and response to telephone calls and lack of sharing of information. Basically, there was lack of accessibility to attorneys to expedite the application process.

Overall, Dawit and Irv observation of the legal system and immigration attorney operation can be regarded as a high-volume, quick-processing operation with profit as driving force. It was characterized by cultural insensitivity/incompetence to deal with clients of diverse background. Dawit and Irv observation shows that immigration attorneys are more preoccupied with "how the judge" would think and how to convince the "immigration judge," than their client worldview and how much they understood what was written in the legal document. It is an upward looking system where the immigration judge is at the top and the client is at the bottom. Every time Dawit and Irv spoke with the legal team they kept saying, "This is what the immigration judge would think about this and that" but never asked how Natsent might think and process those issues discussed or laid out in the legal document. What was clear to Dawit and Irv was that having an attorney was not enough. A client has to be on top of his or her case and at times train their attorneys about how they think about things discussed in the legal document. However, the cultural miscommunication and legal complexity cannot simply be clear to clients and put enough faith on their attorneys. Not alone people like Natsnet with no linguistic and educational proficiency, even a middle class American with a college degree could struggle understanding it. The immigration legal system is very complicated to most people and to get the services that Natsent got is simply beyond the financial capacity of a person seeking asylum or other immigration services. Dawit and Irv raised thousands of dollars and spent thousands of hours of their own time to make this asylum process happen. There are thousands or even millions of genuine asylum seekers and people with other immigration related needs in America that might not have access to such help (see chapter 8 for more details on the financial burden of immigration in the US).

CHAPTER 8. "WE MUST CONTROL THE BORDERS": A KALEIDO-SCOPE OF IMAGES

Natsnet's Images

Not only was Natsnet apprehensive about her own legal and personal problems, especially the rocky relationship with the legal team, but she was also intensely curious about the immigration debate in the larger American society a debate that raised issues that could negatively affect the lives of her children. Until she was granted asylum, she felt herself in jeopardy, and understanding the dynamics of the immigration issue, from an American perspective, was crucial to her own future.

She followed statements about immigration in the presidential debates; she watched television talk shows; she listened in buses, stores, and other public spaces to peoples' conversations. Her still-limited English language ability filtered words and concepts, "hazed" them, one might say, so that much of what she heard was muffled and confusing, like trying to see through a cloud. Often she learned more in these situations by simply watching people's body language. For example, hand gestures tell a lot and listening to the tone of their voices – shrillness is a good clue.

She had one ace in the hole, as the saying goes, one sure resource, and she found this source most informative: the Voice of America's Tigrinya stream that Natsnet could listen to via her friend's computer. While her understanding of the larger political context remained limited, through the VOA broadcasts, and the supplementary things she learned from just listening and observing, she could get the gist, feeling the immigration debate.

Just as it was important for Natsnet to understand, so it was important to her to keep the news of her own status to as small a group as possible within her own inner circle, the *Habesha* community. Orange City was, after all, home to her children and herself. Being an illegal or undocumented immigrant comes with a high degree of stigma; not to be documented is equated with untrustworthiness and invites discrimination.

Natsnet had heard people talking often in hushed tones about how "illegals" have taken American jobs, made American society less safe, and violated national sovereignty. She had heard thoughtless remarks urging the deportation of all undocumented persons from US soil, and wild assertions that such persons were simply criminals, undeserving of any favorable consideration, most certainly never a path to citizenship. More stunning for Natsnent was the elevated rhetoric on immigration going to the extreme on building "walls" in American borders to prevent "illegal migrants" from entering the US. The degree of intensity and the level of emotions that the immigration debate evoked, particularly during the presidential election, frightened Natsnet.

Natsnet knew she had been trafficked to the US by people who were well respected in American diplomatic circles. Even though they were non-citizens, they nevertheless had power, privilege, and influence in this democratic country. And all of these accrued to them despite their denial to their own people the same rights that their elite status granted them at least, in a de facto way, in America. Natsnet had not violated anybody's borders; that she knew with all her heart.

Natsnet dwelt on the statements she heard. In a daydream or maybe it was a nightmare she imagined the stereotype of the "illegal," the undocumented, taken to outlandish proportions. The images portray the invasion of the country by those who illegally crossed American borders, usually with some sort of ill intent, who work here for starvation wages doing menial work washing dishes, picking fruit, cleaning houses and toilets, and the like. They then are thought to send great sums of money as remittances made from these menial jobs back to their respective countries. By so doing, they take jobs from good American workers, eagerly seeking employment in convenience stores and fast-food joints, and somewhat mystically diminishing wages across the board for all.

In Natsnet's daydream or her nightmare the stereotype does not end there, and is taken even further. Undocumented immigrants are portrayed in even more deleterious ways as criminals, members of organized crime, drug dealers, ID-card forgers, petty thieves, armed robbers, and, at times, people who hate America and are committed to terrorist acts. Sometimes, these illegal immigrants are even blamed for the poor educational quality of schools in certain neighborhoods, for the spread of infectious diseases, and for air pollution. In her daydream, Natsnet sees anti-illegal immigration signs posted everywhere she goes. Never mind the ludicrousness of these stereotypes.

While no one could claim that there is not some element of truth in these stereotypes, these behavioral patterns by immigrants are the exceptions rather than the norm. In any community, there are the hopeless who could not stand discrimination and stigmatization. When they lost all the things they dreamt of coming to America to achieve, and became involved in self- destructive and community destroying behaviors. Some might call them criminals, but others also call them a group of people who were pushed by an unfair system that failed to address their problems. No matter how it is construed, their dysfunctional behaviors are not different from those of the general population. They are the product of a society that has the good and the bad, the angel and the devil, the brave and the traitor, and most importantly the poor and the rich. Every society has those life dichotomies that become part of a process of social and economic inequality formation of today.

One way or another, Natsnet knows that she does not fit these biases that are echoed in every part of American society. In fact, she is very much like the general population whose ancestors came here in search of economic opportunity, while escaping oppression in their home countries. When all is evened out, Natsnet is still in search of the same opportunity and freedoms that were offered to the forbears of so many in the general American population. Despite this knowledge, she is always frightened about the whole thing, fearing that the judges and the lawyers handling her case might have the same biases and prejudices of the people in her daydreams.

Tesfa and Daniel Are Growing Up

Natsnet knows very well how grown up her children are, especially her daughter. Natsnet has to hide her immigration status from this American-born daughter. Tesfa, now a precocious third-grader speaks flawless English and is to the distress of many *Habesha*, and to Natsnet's confusion becoming thoroughly Americanized. (She prefers rye bread to *injera*. hamburger to *shiro*, and hotdogs to *qualwaa*!)

Tesfa is also conscious of the American immigration system. At one point, she shared with her mother a disturbing story about a friend in school whose father was arrested and deported because he was living in the United States illegally. Even though Tesfa did not fully understand why he was deported, she told Natsnet how she felt bad for her friend whose father was basically forcefully shipped out of the country because of his immigration status. After hearing Tesfa's story, Natsnet was heartbroken. At the same time, she was very fearful imagining how her and her children's lives would be unalterably dislocated if the same thing were to happen to her.

Tesfa's story only increased the burden of fear that Natsnet bore as well as building a wall between her and her children since there was now a major element of her life that she could not discuss frankly and sincerely with Tesfa and Daniel. "It is hard to be in that situation," Natsnet says, recalling her days as an "illegal" in America. "It's hard to live with limited freedom in the birthplace of freedom," she goes on. Even though the *Habesha* community knew about her immigration status, she could not tell her daughter and her two-year-old son. Natsnet did not want Tesfa and her brother to suffer the stigma, with its pain and suffering, that was attached to her. At the same time, if she told her children, the information could leak beyond the *Habesha* community, placing both her and her children in danger of legal retaliation.

Natsnet's Further Burden

To make matters worse for Natsnet, she also had to explain her immigration status to her parents and extended family back in Eritrea who still needed her help. She sadly recalls that:

> It was very hard to explain to them why I could not visit them in a third country or even send them money during holidays and other family events. In most parts of the world, America is considered as the land of the free and a citadel of justice. It was just impossible for someone living in Eritrea to understand why a country of that stature would not be able to understand my plea for refuge. Most people think if you make it to America, your protection from injustice is a guaranteed fact.

However, this was not what Natsnet got. She still had to fight to get her freedom, and the legal fight was big and expensive, draining her both financially and emotionally. Her family in Eritrea could not understand this, and Natsnet felt her own integrity in her family's eyes has been compromised.

Many times, the whole situation was just too much and too hard for Natsnet. She was quite fed up with the politicization of the whole immigration issue and its failure to address the underlying causes of immigration. It seemed to her that American illegal immigration was always being construed as a problem with Mexico, but in fact it went far beyond that. She, herself, was trafficked here from Saudi Arabia by her "masters." She had escaped her forced confinement by them here in America. By constructing the situation so geopolitically with Mexico, many of the real issues of migration fell by the wayside, while a latent prejudice against persons of color was given flame, and bigotry fueled. The economic realities driving many to become immigrants were simply ignored by the arguments as they are now posed. Natsnet felt that some "talking heads" were simply so far removed from reality, having no understanding of how she saw the world, her everyday existence, and the problems she faced.

Dealing on a daily basis with her own status, Natsnet would have been happy to explain her situation to people holding these biases, but she could not: her fear of deportation and her lack of English-language fluency precluded her joining the debate.

Natsnet struggled with all of these, trying to understand how a nation of immigrants, a land of freedom, found itself unable to deal with issues of immigration and the needs of immigrants like her, just wanting to escape daunting economic hardships and political repression.

Irv's Images

Irv lives in southeastern Utah in the town of Moab with an estimated 2012 population of 5,093. The larger political entity is Grand County with an estimated 2012 population of 9,328. The county's land mass in one and one-half the times of the size of the state of Delaware. It is a big place! Deserts, mountains, and red rock constitute the scenery. A boom-and-bust mining town of copper and uranium Moab is trying to reinvent itself as a tourist destination. Two national parks and one major state park are readily accessible from Moab. The town bills itself as "the mountain biking capital of the world," to boot.

Moab is about 85 percent white. Hispanics constitute the largest proportion of the minority population followed by Native American inhabitants. African-Americans and persons of other races are present in only small numbers. The town has served as a beacon, attracting pilgrims from all parts of the country. These newcomers often make Moab their home, and one can identify distinct strata of intellectually independent sorts who come from "elsewhere." In the '60s, hippies found the town to be a pleasant destination even if they were not welcomed with open arms by the "locals," veterans of the mines, ranchers, and others, many with deep roots in Utah and its Mormon heritage. Artists and photographers, poets and writers followed. In many ways, like most places, Moab is a crucible in which the culture wars are acted out if not actually fought. Newcomers versus locals, "rads" versus Mormons, progressives versus conservatives,"

Given the make of Moab community, few Moab white residents know anything about Africa or African culture. In September 2010 when Dawit and another Eritrean friend, visited Moab, Irv planned a social event a "Gala Africana Party" which turned into an interesting sociological experiment. The invitation to the party invited attendees to compete in an "Africana Contest." The ground rules, as stated in the invitation, follow:

> To enter the seductive Africana Contest, and to compete for a prize, please wear a piece of African attire, sport some African jewelry, or deck yourself in something "just so African." Be innovative and design your own entry! Two prizes will be awarded: one for authenticity and one for originality. Judge Dawit and other Africans present will preside.

The guests were not avid participants. Three or four wore cheap mail-order dashikis, but most came "Moab casual." What was, however, interesting were the comments of invitees before the party. A professional heritage management expert said, "Oh, I'll wear my coconut bra!" It was a great stereotype, but geographical location was a bit wrong! Another guest, a college graduate, asked, "Is it still 'in' to come naked?" A professional artist said, "I'll come dressed as a Massai warrior with just a loincloth." Another invitee, with a graduate degree, proclaimed, "Most women in Africa don't wear tops." a retired Moab resident, said, "He was going to wear his wife's African dress," a gift brought from an African country by a friend. Irv loved his community so much and loved each of them but the community understanding about Africa was very limited and sometimes their limited knowledge is drawn from a stereotypical imagination of the continent. Irv passionately remembers how people from his community are willing to help to any important cause he and Dawit were planning in doing in the Horn of Africa. Their generosity and willingness to help inspired Irv everyday but at the same time, Irv wanted his community to understand the continents social, geographical, and natural beauty as well. Irv insisted that the African continent should not be defined by stereotypes or gross generalizations that are so common in Moab and many parts of the United States.

It is not just African culture of which most Moab residents are unfamiliar but immigrants in general. In an offhanded way, Irv tells of one of his encounters with an elderly woman, a Moabite transplanted from elsewhere.

BACKGROUND SECTION NO. 6:

A Sign of the Times: Irv's Encounter with Victoria

It was mid-afternoon. I was hungry and not particularly interested in meeting up with any overly talkative Moabites. The town is loaded with them.

I stopped in Fluto's, the local outlet of a major fast-food chain. Heading to the counter, a voice called out, "Irv! Irv!" The local nonagenarian matriarch, doyen of the town's Episcopal bluebloods, continued, "It's so good to see you; won't you join me?"

Oh, shit, I was trapped. I had no alternative but to sit down at her booth and watch her pick at her omelet in her very proper bicultural way: southern upbringing laced with lots of New England quality time!

We made a good effort at small talk and I began telling her about "the case," Natsnet's, that had been keeping me busy for the last several years. When Victoria heard the word "immigrant" and "asylum," she became animated. "But how did she get 'eeeee-nnn'?", she said two times over, pronouncing "in" as if it were a two-syllable word, and enunciating each of the imagined syllables. This was followed by a bit of *de rigueur* pabulum, the theme of which was, "We've got to control the border."

Victoria lives with her three children and son-in-law, a local bigot who has been infected with the highly contagious attitude set seeping (or "creeping") across the border from Arizona. To say he dislikes, is bigoted against, or just plain despises – immigrants, is an understatement. Fortunately for Ms. Natsnet, she's not Mexican, hence the stigma against her in the son-in-law's eyes is an iota less.

I continued with my story. Victoria continued to look agitated. Finally, in a moment of compromise after all, she has known me for well over 12 years she said: "Well, maybe she does really want to better herself, but we've got to control the border." Etc., etc., etc.

Victoria continued to pick at her omelet, prepared for her by a young Mexican guy, an immigrant, of course. The mess she would leave at her table would be cleaned up by a middle-aged Mexican busboy, who held two jobs, in addition to his exalted position at Fluto's. (I wondered how many natural-born Americans both of these guys had beaten out to get these jobs?) I wondered if either of those men wanted "to improve themselves."

In a complete *non se·qui·tur,* Victoria leaned toward me and told me about her hobby of genealogy. She said that in each generation of her family, there was a genealogist. I asked her how far back she could trace her family. She told me, with an obvious smirk of pride, that her family went back to Charlemagne. I resisted asking, "How did you all get 'eeeee-nnn'?" Then she confided that she and a college friend had reminded each other that the President was "half white." Conspiratorially, she lowered her voice and told me as one white to another that it was his other half that was causing him problems.

Mercifully, Victoria stopped picking at her food leaving more on her plate uneaten, and thus wasted, than many people in the world eat in an entire day and the conversation ended. I left.

The whole incident indicated to me that distressing lack of thought that we bourgeois Americans have given to immigration, the policies and politics associated with it, and the personal aspects of being an "immigrant."

Irv, himself, was a former college professor who found the confines of the ivory tower oppressive. He began a career in civil rights with a stint in the 1970s in the National Urban

League. In 1974, he was recruited to a civil rights operation in the U.S. Department of Transportation in Washington.

Dawit's Images

Living far away, in a different part of the United States, from Natsnet, Dawit was then living in Gainesville, Florida. Gainesville is lively liberal university town, home to the sprawling University of Florida, surrounded by multiple-use urban areas of various socioeconomic levels. In 2012, Gainesville was estimated to have 126,047 residents. The surrounding Alachua County, much of it rural in nature, is home to an estimated 251,417 persons. In both political entities, whites predominate although African Americans are present in sizeable numbers.

In the university community, most people are supportive of the rights of undocumented immigrants both in the state and nationally. This community has always stood to protect the interests and the needs of undocumented immigrants. Whenever there is a discussion about immigration, the university community can be counted on to launch a demonstration in support of the immigrant underdogs the undocumented and others. There is a high degree of support in the Gainesville university community for immigrant rights and the establishment of a path to citizenship. However, Natsnet does not live here and does not feel the support Dawit sees in his community. What she sees in the state and city she lives in is different and many times could be characterized as mixed.

Like Irv, Dawit received support, criticism, and nonchalance for his role in Natsnet's freedom. The nonchalance came mainly from the local community outside of the University setting who seemed, at many times, oblivious to the world. In his efforts to support and assist Natsnet, Dawit had a great deal of support and praise from students and other friends associated with the university in Gainesville. To more effectively help Natsnet, Dawit sought the guidance and counsel of his Latino friends. Pedro is one of Dawit's friends from Mexico who studies migrant workers in the United States and works with different organizations that help undocumented immigrants. Pedro discussed with Dawit the kind of experiences common to a lot of undocumented migrant workers in the United States and the struggles they face to make a living. Pedro's wife also works on immigration matters, especially with the Latina American diaspora, and was a great source of advice for Dawit as Natsnet's application for asylum was being built. Dawit also received a lot of praise and support from people outside of the University of Florida who strongly felt the struggles and challenges undocumented workers and immigrants face. One of Dawit's friend, Lacey and her family, were very supportive of Dawit's efforts to help Natsnet throughout her ordeal, and were always available to help Natsnet, both financially and morally.

One night after a good talk with Dawit, Lacey said:

> I feel the struggle of Natsnet is similar to what my forebears went through when they arrived from Europe, escaping persecution and discrimination because of who they were. If America gave them opportunity and protection during those difficult days, then Natsnet deserves the same.

This was an encouraging statement and an effective summary of Dawit's sentiments. Dawit also got praise and encouragement from his own professors for his work to address the needs of asylum seekers and other undocumented Eritrean immigrants in the United States including Natsnet.

In other ways, Gainesville is a living embodiment of the culture wars that plague the US on so many fronts. The liberal University of Florida is one site of Gainesville. The town is also the residence of the well-publicized and vitriolic Qur'an-burning "man of God", who created a global media frenzy by planning to burn a Qur'an in public. From a college-town downtown area, to the cultural events held at the University, to the sophisticated restaurants of the southwestern part of the city, to the affluent suburbs, scenes and attitudes reminiscent of *Mississippi Burning* are never more than a 20 minute drive as is the proximate ghettoized east side of the town.

It was from this latter perspective that an unpleasant reaction from one of his classmates at the school of public health at the University of Florida emanated. Dawit's critic's name is Anderson and comes from a small rural town outside of Gainesville. After he learned that Dawit was helping an undocumented immigrant, Anderson showed his protest to Dawit by saying:

> You are helping people that have broken American laws and illegally crossed our borders. You are helping criminals who are working using fake IDs, and driving cars without drivers' licenses and killing innocent Americans. Dawit this is not right! People like those whom you are helping should be deported without any precondition and notice. We are tired of criminals and we do not want to see them here anymore. Despite the reasons why she came here, America should not be responsible for people like her and neither should America tolerate their actions.

In these images, we can see a deep array of kaleidoscope of attitudes and opinions, hopes and fears, surrounding the whole issue of immigration that reflects today's American immigration debate.

CHAPTER 9. ANTHROPOLOGICAL AND POLITICAL PERSPECTIVES OF AMERICAN ASYLUM SYSTEM

Natsnet's personal story, the legal battle she faced, and the web of personal problems she had to deal with attracted a natural human reaction from Dawit and Irv. Natsnet's situation cried for the kind of help that they could give, and as we have seen in the last chapter, they tried to render. Most importantly, it provided Dawit and Irv with the opportunity to look at the systemic problems Natsnet faced from their respective disciplinary perspectives: cultural anthropology and political science.

Four major areas of concern stand out:

- Economic bars to accessing the asylum process and judicial remedies
- Relative powerlessness of the petitioner or the asylum-seeker as supplicant
- The critical importance of cross-cultural communication and miscommunication in the asylum process

- The nebulous ubiquity of politics in the asylum process

Economic Bars to Accessing the Asylum Process and Judicial Remedies

Accessing the asylum-system costs a considerable sum of money that most asylum-seekers simply do not have. Almost by necessity, an attorney must be engaged, and attorneys' fees can be a hurdle many cannot overcome. Lacking "papers", this is the final reward of the asylum system; asylum seekers are likely to be unemployed; if they are employed, there is a high probability that they are doing so illegally, holding only the most marginal of jobs. Tapping the resources of the petitioner's social network, those who are likely to be in impoverished positions themselves, is often the only way an asylum-seeker can raise money. Doing so, places the applicant in the role of a beggar.

Because the petitioner lacks a steady stream of income or other resources, the applicant is forced to bargain for low-cost asylum services. Natsnet's first two attorneys are a case in point. Both were secured at bargain rates, and both gave her less than satisfactory service. When Dawit and Irv sought out her last attorneys, cost was a major consideration, although this was somewhat mitigated by their experience and judgment in navigating complex social systems. They had the skills that Natsnet did not, to secure a "good" attorney at a reasonable price and to, themselves, dig out sources of aid and to guide Natsnet to charitable sources of support.

Relative Powerlessness of the Petitioner

In any asylum proceeding, the petitioner is almost by definition without power, a supplicant, virtually a pawn in the game. The immigration attorney, the gatekeeper, holds the keys to the proceeding itself, out of which will come the symbolic heavenly kingdom of "asylum granted," or the hell of "asylum denied." In the previous chapter, we examined the legal team's role as hegemon when it came to Natsnet and we suggest that this role was systemically generated. Even though the case was about her, and her future was on the line, Natsnet constantly chafed at her subordinate role.

Moreover, the turf on which the process takes place involves sanctuary-like deliberation rooms. A robed official, the judge, usually sits in an elevated seat that is tiered above the assembled players who sit as supplicants beneath, or in a well, to the front of the judge. A stilted and archaic dialect of English is used with seemingly antediluvian rules of procedure prevailing. A piously deferential and respectful style almost like a stage play is carried on throughout. All of this is steeped in the emblems of state power. The judge is flanked by the national and state ensigns. Generally, the Great Seal or a similar symbol is prominently emblazoned on the paneling in front of the judge's "bench" or mounted on the wall behind the judge. For the individual petitioner, this, indeed, is a formidable array of state power emphasizing the applicant's lesser or supplicant status.

The Critical Importance of Cross-Cultural Communication and Miscommunication in the Asylum Process

As social scientists, we well know that reality is a social construct, built and conditioned by culture and custom, social status and class, and time and place. The asylum process reflects this general proposition and is characterized by a lack of cross-cultural perspectives on immigration and other legal matters. For example, medical anthropologists who examine how different cultures view and experience illnesses have made similar observations. Arthur Kleinman's work with spirit possession in traditional Chinese cultural belief systems is a classic example, showing how people of one culture experience and perceive illnesses in different ways from people in other cultures and from biomedical-trained physicians or psychiatrists (Kleinman 1981). Anne Fadiman, in *The Spirit Catches You and You Fall Down*, does the same for a Hmong child, a Laotian immigrant, living in California demonstrating how doctors and parents view the child's health problem quite differently (Fadiman 1998). It explores some of the cultural collision that happen between doctors and patients of different cultural background.

Further examples of the embodiment of the norms of western culture and epistemology in the American asylum process are many. These include linear reasoning and precise time sequences, logically developed according to sound Aristotelian principles, as critical components of any judicial process. Contradicting one's self in relating a chronology simple inconsistent remembrance of dates can equal perjury in the legal sense. The system itself enshrines the rule of "one strike and you're out," and this is often the reason asylum cases are "thrown out" and their petitioners' hopes dashed, and fears justified.

The legal system and training "in the law" is so structured that it makes it very difficult for those whose work it is for those who make it "work" to accommodate other cultural thought processes. Even though the investigative process is complex and thorough and is seen as "objective" the reasoning process of attorneys and judges is embedded in a particular cultural reality. Anything outside the cultural perspectives of the judges who heard Natsnet's case, or the culture in which the law is based, was understood very poorly or not at all. Objectivity therefore becomes a very subjective concept.

Consider the social characteristics that Natsnet brought to her "encounter" with justice. First, on a continuum from "orality" to "literary," Natsnet is a clearly an "oral" person. That is, she is much more adept and psychologically comfortable speaking, rather than writing. The latter is a mode of communication with which she is not comfortable. However, the asylum process involves masses of written documents required by law, and this body of work remained a mystery to Natsnet.

Natsnet's language, Tigrinya, is a member of the Semitic family; her knowledge of English, at least at that time, was quite limited. She thought in Tigrinya and reasoned in Semitic ways. Semitic thought patterns, as opposed to Western thought patterns, are basically different, impeding mutual understanding and communication. Throughout our work with Natsnet, we were reminded of the Hebrew picture language of the biblical Old Testament versus the more linear Western thought patterns of the New Testament. Semitic thought unfolds in more "circular" patterns than the "linear" English language. Also, patterns of logic and expression are quite different.

For Natsnet, feasts and other holy days in the Orthodox religious calendar were of critical importance and aligned with the annual cycle of birth, life, and death. Events were "remembered" in clusters, related to this yearly cycle. Stories were told by describing these clusters, each of which was linked to the other in some generic – but probably not linear way. When all the clusters were recounted, the narrative was complete.

Natsnet's sense of time was radically different from the American "norm." From the beginning, her culture did not teach her to be obsessed with time. (She did not even own a wristwatch until she came to Orange City.) In the end, from her point of view, time really just didn't matter all that much. In her background, the rising of the sun, relatively regular in areas near the Equator, was the beginning of the day, or twelve o'clock in the morning. Its setting was the end of the day, also at twelve o'clock. (Western visitors to her country sometimes confused her by calling these times six o'clock in the morning and afternoon.) The calendar in which Natsnet was raised and "thought" had 13 months: twelve were long months and one was a short month (This is, of course, a modified version of the Julian calendar although it goes much deeper than just that). Westerners thought of time differently. Like other things, the concept of time is a cultural one, and different societies and cultures understand and use time differently.

This means the asylum applicant has to learn how to operate with a "foreign" reckoning of time and sequencing of events. For Natsnet, although she remembered quite well her birth date, the year she graduated from high school, the date of her leaving Eritrea, or her entry date to the US, translating these into Western terms was always a challenge, especially for events quite distant in the past.

In 1986, Walter Kälin, in "Troubled Communication: Cross-Cultural Misunderstanding in the Asylum-Hearing," outlined some culturally related problems in western legal systems. He pointed out the manner of expression in the courtroom is an important cultural element that could potentially create some form of mistrust or misunderstanding. Manner of expression is a cross-cultural phenomenon where different cultures show the same kind of expression but these could "mean" differently. Norms of interpersonal contact are different. In some cultures, eye contact is disrespectful; in

American culture, it is a sign of sincerity and truthfulness. Physical space between speakers connotes different meanings in different cultures. Lateral head shaking doesn't always mean "no"; in some cultures, it signifies agreement. Kälin shows that even "a lie" and "Truth" are culturally conditioned concepts (Walter Kälin 1986).

Kälin stresses the role of the interpreter who shares a culture with the petitioner and translates that culture for the court, acting as a mediator between two cultures or as a broker of one culture to another. He shows that oftentimes language translation does not equal cultural translation.

However, Dawit and Irv's experience with several lawyers who worked on Eritrean asylum cases, and Dawit and Irv's interview with attorneys and federal judges, showed that these anthropological thought processes are absent in most cases. The law is still culturally linear and the processes implementing it suffer from the lack of a cross-cultural perspective. Simply put, the legal system expects defendants to operate in American cultural thought process and construct their cases based on those cultural rules. America is one of the most diverse societies in the world and usually pride itself being that way, however, its legal systems, medical system, and other public service sectors at times fail to match and accommodate the needs of the diverse cultural values that exist.

BACKGROUND SECTION NO. 7:

Cross-Cultural Observations by a Court Translator

My name is Daniel T. Abraham. I am originally from the central region of Eritrea but born raised in Addis Ababa Ethiopia.

My first languages were Amharic and Tigrinya, and I learned English, Russian, and French during my schooling, especially my years at Addis Abba University. I was deported to Eritrea during the 1997-2000 Ethiopian-Eritrean border war. In early 2000's, I was fortunate enough to get a job with the Eritrean Ministry of Foreign Affairs doing writing and translating for the Office of the Foreign Minister. In August of 2003 I was posted to an Eritrean foreign diplomatic mission in the west, and also doing writing and translating duties.

My political loyalties were very much opposed to the government for which I was working and my situation became intolerable. I was harassed and threatened. My family's house in Asmara was searched and my computer seized. I had to leave and I sought political asylum in the US. It took about a year, but I was granted asylum and I entered a graduate program at a well-regarded US university. To support myself, I worked as a court translator for the federal judiciary in New York City, Washington DC, Philadelphia, Boston, and Baltimore.

My experiences in the court were very revealing and illustrate the cultural difficulties and challenges non-English speaker immigrants face in the United States. Let me give you a few examples of intercultural communication gone wrong:

My first example took place about a year ago, and involved the interaction among the client, judge, and attorney in a court hearing involving the wrongful death of an Ethiopian man about a year before this incident. In the trial, the widow, also Ethiopian was called to testify. Since the couple had been in the US only a few years, and used Amharic at home, her English was lacking. She testified in Amharic and I translated.

Inquiring into the status of her relationship with her dead husband, the judge asked the woman if her husband had been "seeing other women or had history of previous affair." The woman began to weep. The judge did not back off. He then asked her if she had a boyfriend or if she was currently dating. The woman cried even harder. The judge did not seem to understand that this was simply a culturally inappropriate question asked in a way that, to the woman, was crass and obnoxious. I understood the woman's point of view completely because of my cultural affinity with her.

While the judge may have had sound legal reason for his line of questioning, from the woman's point of view, these queries were intrusive and absolutely inappropriate. From her cultural perspective, the dead are sacred and should not be brought into social scrutiny that involve any moral failure. Similarly, from her cultural perspective, it is taboo for a widow to date or have a boyfriend. In fact, when and if she decided to remarry, she needed the permission of her in-laws and her own family and other close relatives.

The scene was absolutely awful: the women kept crying hysterically. The tension in the room started to get high. The woman was upset and started to throw some verbal punches at the judge. She felt she was insulted and treated like "a prostitute." She said to the judge "I am not a prostitute and my deceased husband needs to rest in peace. He was a good husband, father, and brother."

Her lawyer, a native-born American didn't understand what was happening and, although he wanted to protect his client, he seemed clueless about what to do. The judge never understood why this woman was crying, why she was angry and unhappy. The judge felt he was doing the right legal thing and doing it in an unbiased and neutral manner. The bottom line was simple: there was a complete lack of communication between the judge and the woman. Of course, I could not speak out; my role was just to interpret what was said on both sides.

Another example, I went to an immigration hearing where a man who currently lives in the United States wanted to bring his daughter to the US to join him. His daughter was in Ethiopia, but he sent her an invitation to join him. The embassy in Ethiopia refused to give her a visa to come to the United States to reunite with the father. The man appealed his case to the immigration courts here in the United States to bring his daughter to the US. The American law system views someone aged 22 as independent and on his/her own but to this Ethiopian man, his daughter will still be his dependent as long as she is not married. American culture views that a child is no more considered dependent after a certain age limit (between 18-22) while in the Ethiopian a child is considered dependent until that person gets married.

The immigration judge tried to explain the immigration rules with regards to family reunion to this man, but the Ethiopian would not understand it because according to him his daughter is not married and she still is considered dependent. This man's understanding of a dependent is shaped by his culture and social norms in Ethiopia. Again the judge informed him that she will not be able to join him based on the family reunion immigration clause, but the judge gave him alternative means that would enable her to come to the United States. While the judge did not do anything wrong here, it shows the lack of communication that emanates from cultural differences between judges/attorneys and their clients from other cultures.

These examples illustrate how the American legal system, and the training of its functionaries, fail to address or accommodate cultural differences. These are not deliberate, but are products of a lack of cross-cultural and geopolitical understanding. Understanding and sensitivity to cultural differences is critical to providing a fair trial to people who desperately need political protection and justice. Cultural competence is a prerequisite for a fair and just system.

The Nebulous Ubiquity of Politics in the Asylum Process

Key players in the political asylum process immigration attorneys agreed unanimously that "politics" plays an important role in asylum decisions. "They just know" was a phrase we heard over and over in our interviews, not only from immigration attorneys, but also from others who were central players in the asylum process. Through the asylum process, decisions are made which allocate values, "goodies", for which people and groups strive. These are decisions in which parties, and the larger sociopolitical interests they reflect, have real and intense stakes. Hence, asylum is political process, however ephemeral those politics may be. According to Rosenbrum and Salehyan (2004), both norms (humanitarian need) and national interest have to be met for a successful asylum application. The authors argue that national interest is not fixed and they change with geopolitical dynamics and US interests. For example, the asylum process before and after the cold War is not the same. Therefore, politics plays an important role in denying or granting asylum.

Similarly, Dawit and Irv interviews with former judges confirm that asylum applicants from a country held in aversion by the United States government are perceived and the empirical data support (UNHCR, 2013 asylum data) to have a better chance at winning asylum than those from more highly regarded countries. Citizens from Iran, Somalia, Eritrea, and

China were the leading asylum applicants and recipients in the US and Europe in 2013 (UNHCR 2013). Immigration litigation is harder for those from "good" states and easier for those from "bad" states. A good measure of the "goodness" or "badness" of another nation state is it's ranking on the State Department's human rights, religious freedom, and trafficking annual reports. The lower a state's ranking that is, the worse it is in its human rights or religious toleration practices the better the chances for a positive outcome from an asylum applicant from that state. The key asylum players agreed that the process for those from "bad' countries was "easier," and petitioners from those countries were more likely to be answered with a grant of asylum. On the other hand, for those from countries in the good graces of the US, achieving a favorable decision was a trickier, but not impossible, accomplishment.

So, how does the current US regime's political line becomes known among the players? How is it transmitted? Of course, the State Department reports are a matter of record as are the public statements of key governmental officials. We also saw evidence of the perception that in the preparation of the State Department's annual reports, politics also played a role. For example, one immigration attorney spoke of the need "to go behind these reports, to a reputable NGO to get the true story." Policy offices are an integral part of any agency, including those with actors in the asylum process, and are well aware of the content of these Department of State reports.

Recruitment into high federal positions is, in part, preconditioned on a person's abilities. The ability to "read signs" or "read the tea leaves" is one of the skills-sets that make a candidate more sought after. This same filtering takes place in the promotional process within governmental agencies. Perhaps in the initial recruitment process, and later in the promotional process, those who "don't just know or get it" are passed over for elevation into key roles, and those who "do just know and get it" advance. Interestingly, almost all of the attorney respondents, when pushed on this subject about a party line, essentially would say something like, "You just know." The authors asked how one just knew, but no real answers were forthcoming. This is why we call the ubiquity of politics "nebulous."

Dawit and Irv interviewed five former judges and other legal professionals and none of them could tell that the political line was in any way dictated or laid out by something like a *ukase* or similar means. While none of the judges whom Dawit and Irv interviewed admitted that any aspect of their decisions were motivated by outside political considerations, or ever admitted that politics played a role in the asylum process, clearly a look at their overall decision-making patterns showed the good-state/bad-state dichotomy. One judge whom Dawit and Irv interviewed did, at one point in the conversation, state that "[o]f course, I knew the line." He quickly reverted to the typical judicial line that his job was the application of the law to factual situations – the simple laying out the facts against a rule a very mechanical view. The authors suggest that in asylum decision-making, much more is going on.

Overall, Natsnet's case raises critical academic and intellectual challenges to the asylum system, especially for attorneys specializing in immigration affairs and in the structuring of the asylum process itself. While working with Natsnet's case, the authors understood they were dealing with a small group of legal professionals; however, their interviews with judges, attorneys, and paralegal professionals concur with their observations.

CHAPTER 10. VICTORY AT LAST

In Chapter 7, the critical role immigration attorneys play in the asylum process is obvious. Even more important roles are played by immigration judges. Irv, with his political science background, and Dawit, with his training in cultural anthropology, examined the literature on the socioeconomic and cultural backgrounds of immigration judges and the possible impacts these variables may have on the decisions judges make. In particular, the words of the final arbiter of Natsnet's case, an African-born woman, with diverse training both in Africa and the United States, are examined in some detail as is the impact that this judge's background may have had on Natsnet's final victory. Background, experience, and cultural factors all play a role in immigration decision making.

Preparatory Phase

Now that the orders for Natsnet to leave the country were lifted because of the changed-country-conditions argument, the second phase of the proceedings to petition for actual asylum began. We went through many of the steps for this second phase which lasted several months as we had done for the first. Irv prepared expert testimony; Dawit worked diligently with Natsnet and Irv. The same judge who had denied asylum to Natsnet years earlier, would preside.

By this time, Natsnet had been through about as much as she could take. As we saw earlier, she had found an Eritrean Orthodox congregation in Orange City, and she continued with vigor her activities within the parish. Her priest truly cared for Natsnet and led the congregation in its collective support of Natsnet. While it might have been a cocoon sheltering Natsnet from the realities of American life, it also was an extraordinary source of succor for her. During the second phase of Natsnet's proceedings, she and her children stayed in the rectory with her priest and his housekeeper.

Early on in this phase of the proceedings Natsnet's father, Berhane, had contracted a serious kidney disease and was hospitalized in an Asmara clinic that passed for a hospital in Eritrea. The diagnosis was not good: Berhane required surgery to save his life, and that procedure could not be performed in Eritrea. In such cases, patients with the necessary means as Berhane had would travel to Italy, the former colonial power, or recently to Sudan where the surgery could be performed with relative ease. In order to get to Italy, Berhane needed the Eritrean government to grant him an exit permit for which he applied while still in the Asmara clinic.

The First Hearing

Natsnet's asylum hearing was scheduled in November. Judge Housum-Yetter was in one of her no-nonsense moods and she was greatly disappointed by the legal team's presentation. She did not hesitate to express herself. In hindsight, Judge Housum-Yetter may have been showing great restraint and perhaps even signaling her decision when she postponed the asylum hearing for another four months. In her most judicial voice, tinged with her African lilt, she told attorneys, "I want everything to be in order in this case: every *t* crossed; every *i* dotted. Put it in better order! Do you hear me?" The Attorneys followed Judge Housum-Yetter's advice while all of us, especially Natsnet, waited apprehensively for the final hearing and outcome. The holidays that year were not the festive time that all of the players were hoping for.

During the critical week before Natsnet's hearing, Natsenet's priest learned through his sources in Eritrea that the Eritrean government had not issued the necessary travel document to allow Berhane to travel to Europe for the surgery that he needed to live. Because of the delay of travel permit, he died just three days before Natsnet's make or break hearing before Judge Housum-Yetter. Dawit learned of Berhane's death and informed all the people involved in her case. The decision was made to keep this from Natsnet, asking her priest to tell her this devastating news after the final hearing was over.

Previously, after the defection of Natsnet's brother Yohannes (pseudonym) from the Eritrean army to seek refugee status in Europe, the father had been forced out of his liquor business through government denial of his application for a renewal of his license to operate. Similar story and government action against families of military evaders has been well documented by several reports (Kibreab 2009, UN Report of the Commission of Inquiry on Human Rights in Eritrea, 2015). Yohannes was also a member of the Medhane Alem Movement and was doing his national service as an army recruit when he was persecuted for his religious beliefs, thus prompting his defection to Europe. There was a clear pattern of persecution here. The Eritrean government's close scrutiny of members of its diaspora, and retaliation against dissenters and their families is as well known, as the state's horrendous prison conditions and systematic torture of dissidents. The sins of Yohannes and Natsnet were ever-present in the eyes of the Eritrean state.

The Second Hearing

Finally, in mid-February of the next year, Natsnet's hearing before Judge Housum-Yetter began. Judge Housum-Yetter was herself an immigrant to the US, growing up in Africa and having studied law in United States and, after becoming an American citizen, here in the US. Her career in the US took her from the practice of immigration law to an immigration judgeship. From all that she had done, she was very much the epitome of a transnational citizen.

"It's over!": As soon as the hearing was called to order, Nastnet's attorneys asked for a private conference in the judge's chambers with the judge and the government attorneys. She informed the party of Natsnet's father's death. Judge Housum-Yetter was stony faced. With all that Natsnet had experienced, Judge Housum Yetter was taken aback. The retaliation demonstrated by the Eritrean government confirmed Natsnet's fears and made her argument for asylum unassailable. The government attorneys were silent when they heard of the political and human right conditions in Eritrea. The court was reconvened. In a simple statement, Judge Housum-Yetter approved Natsnet's petition for asylum. The case was finished; Natsnet had won.

All that morning, Irv was on-call to give testimony by phone. Dawit was teaching. One of Natsnet's attorneys called Irv later in that morning, saying simply "It's over! We're done." Natsnet came on the phone crying joyfully. Irv cried too. Natsnet had won her bid for political asylum. Finally, the case had been won, but at a terrible price. Natsnet was told by the priest about her father's death only after the final hearing was over. Natsnet cried again, only these were tears of mourning.

Looking Back; Looking Ahead

Natsnet's pursuit for the legal freedom to stay in the US was finally achieved. It was a battle that Natsnet and her supporters had fought for years. It was a righteous war for freedom just as her own country, many years before, had fought a righteous war for its independence. However, Natsnet's striving to be free was not over. The years of trauma and life challenges had taken their toll. Her years in Saudi Arabia weigh heavily upon her. Natsnet is still fighting to gain her freedom, freedom to be able to pursue her life with independence, without depending on others, and the freedom to express her thoughts and emotions in English, the language of her host country. Natsnet continues to seek freedom from the uncertainty that comes with having no health insurance, permanent home, or other necessities of life in a country where opportunities are rationed by education and degree of cultural assimilation. Natsnet also continues to seek freedom from a life of constant worry about her Eritrean homeland with its harsh living conditions. Her family there will be under constant threat of reprisal for the actions of Natsnet and Yohannes, so long as the current regime rules (UN Report of the Commission of Inquiry on Human Rights in Eritrea, 2015, Kibreab 2009).

She knows that she will never be able to return to Eritrea. The stories of oppression told by those who have escaped that land are harrowing. These range from abduction by traffickers assisted by high military officers; the deaths of refugees seeking freedom by crossing the Sinai Desert; the drowning in the Mediterranean Sea of refuges trying to get to Europe using small boats; and much more. A UN body, mandated to monitor Somalia and Eritrea on arms trafficking, report that Eritrean military Generals and officers are implicated in the abduction and trafficking of people and smuggle them to Sudan en route to Israel through Sinai and Libya en route to Italy. In a report submitted to the European Union, the Guardian newspaper made similar claims based on two Swedish human right researchers and activists.

Natsnet also hears about the continuing deterioration of political and social conditions in Eritrea where her mother and siblings still live. Movement is restricted; exit permits are regularly withheld; checkpoints are everywhere; arbitrary arrests are common; privacy is nonexistent; and the government is omnipresent and omnipotent (Bozzini, 2011, UN Report of the Commission of Inquiry on Human Rights in Eritrea, 2015). Basic freedoms are denied; health and educational services are deteriorating rapidly (Bozzini 2011). Several of her family and friends have died because of lack of basic medical supplies; children are malnourished; the same malnutrition causes babies to be stillborn or to have major mental impairments.

Natsnet also hears of government officials racing against time to accumulate enough money in foreign accounts before the government crumples. Many thousands of political prisoners languish in secret Eritrean jails (Connell 2005, Human Right Watch 2009). More importantly Natsnet worries about the very real possibility of chaos, instability, and violence when the one-man regime suddenly collapses. It is a country where there is an absolute lack of institutions and rule of law

(UN Report of the Commission of Inquiry on Human Rights in Eritrea, 2015).

Natsent has also heard the horrifying news of the disappearance of close to 400 Eritrean migrants in a shipwreck near Lampedusa, Italy (The largest human loss in the Mediterranean Sea in recent memory), while seeking freedom from the grip of the Eritrean regime. There has been so much human tragedy at sea and the Maltese prime minster claims "The Mediterranean Sea is turning into a cemetery" (BBC, 12 oct.2013). Natsnet has heard of Eritrean migrants killed in Sinai by merciless organized traffickers but this particular incident at sea, she says "aches her hearts". She lost close family members in this tragic incident. She thought things would be a lot better now than the time she left Eritrea. However, things have even gotten worse and people are (especially the youth) are leaving the country in droves. According to a 2014 UNHCR report the number of refugees in Europe from Eritrea during the first ten months of 2014 has tripled. In 2014 alone 37,000 Eritreans sought asylum in Europe. Despite the shoot and kill policy of the Eritrean government, about 1,000 young people between the ages of 18-24 are leaving Eritrea every month to Sudan alone (UNCHR 2014). The same report also indicated an even greater number of Eritrean fleeing to Ethiopia every month. In October of 2014 alone 5000 Eritrean young men and women crossed to Ethiopia.

Natsnet can never be free of the Eritrean government. Eritrean citizenship is not renounceable. Its diaspora agents maintain effective surveillance of the Eritrean diaspora (UN Report of the Commission of Inquiry on Human Rights in Eritrea, 2015). A two-percent tax is levied on all Eritreans living abroad. Other fees and surcharges are imposed and payment is coerced by the regime's agents in the diaspora. Scare tactics and intimidation are used. To Natsnet, these people embody the nightmares that all Eritrean youth experience. For Natsent freedom means to live in America, free of the Eritrean regime.

Natsnet has won her asylum in America, but she is haunted by the regime in Eritrea. It constrains and binds her. She wants to live a normal life where she can recover from her traumas. The smiles of happiness she achieved from her legal struggle are counterbalanced by all of these fears and apprehensions including the linguistic, cultural, and economic barriers she continuously encounters here in America.

However, at a personal level Natsnet is hopeful, because one victory brings another. She feels she now has a stepping-stone from where she can launch a successful new life in America. She is hopeful and tremendously appreciative of the help that she has received from her American supporters. Her victory is not just hers, but a victory for all the people around her. She wants to maintain this success and fulfill her dream of achieving her full freedom.

CHAPTER 11. A NEW LIFE AWAITS NATSNET'S FUTURE

Natsnet's Struggle to Keep Her Family Together

In many ways, life in Orange City was difficult for Natsnet, especially in maintaining the integrity of her mother-daughter/son relationship with Tesfa and Daniel. Her ex-boyfriend's behavior with Tesfa and Daniel continued, complicating Natsnet's relationship with her children. On his every other weekend with the children, he lavished them with special treats that every child loves ice cream, French fries, burgers, delighting in comparing his generosity to Natsnet's "stinginess." Natsnet tried her best to see that the children had a healthy diet and the treats her ex gave were simply not part of such a diet, except on special occasions. For her ex-boyfriend and his campaign of alienation, every occasion was special. It seemed as if he were constantly trying to turn the children against her.

Natsnet was fortunate that her *Habesha* community owned a small basement apartment, which they rented to her at a very reasonable price. The apartment had a living room with combined kitchen and dining space, a small room where Tesfa and Daniel slept, and a separate, larger room for Natsnet. It was located on a quiet street just off one of Orange City's busiest thoroughfares containing six lanes with speeding cars going east and west. A supermarket was nearby, quite within walking distance, and Natsnet's Ethiopian friend, Aster, often visited. Once in a while, Natsnet and Aster would share a drink of *tej*, Ethiopian honey wine, that Aster and her husband made at home. In a few months, Natsnet would find a way to get to the county animal shelter, and adopt the cat that Tesfa and Daniel was so longing for!

Also Natsnet had part-time work at a used car lot where she cleaned cars, restrooms, and the office, kept the vending machines stocked, and did other needed odd chores. The lot was owned by an immigrant from Pakistan, a man named Syed, who was generous and hardworking, and who had hardscrabbled his way up the economic ladder that faces so many newcomers. Syed has a master's degree in business administration from Aga Khan University in Karachi, but his search for professional work met only closed doors. Foreign degrees, especially from non-western countries, counted for little in America. He had been forced to do it all the hard way and he did not slack in sharing his good fortune with others who were struggling now, as he had struggled in his first years in the US.

Natsnet's Cultural Values

Natsnet had grown up in a solidly middle class family within traditional *Habesha* culture and her values reflected this, even in America. Despite Tesfa's Americanization, she was determined to pass the values on to her and her growing brother. Strong family ties with an extended family structure and sense of reciprocal obligations among family members is a key cultural component of Eritrean life. She would not lose this here.

Natsnet had a deep sense of her Eritrean cultural roots and knowledge of the antiquity of that culture. She was proud of her historical past and had a deep appreciation of its thousand years old roots. In addition, Natsnet recognized, and was intensely proud of Eritrean artistic and literary traditions and she had a strong attachment to things traditionally "Eritrean." In her own way, her apartment was decorated in a typically Eritrean manner. She was especially proud of her wall hangings, especially one depicting the Holy Family's flight to Egypt, Al Khulafa Al Rashiudin, Eritrean biggest mosque in Asmara, Saint Mary Church in Asmara, arts from the Eritrean liberation struggle, and Eritrean famous Archaeological sites of Qohyaito and Metera in Southern Eritrea that predates Christianity.

Natsnet's keen sense of national and ethnic pride that was often seen by other Africans as bordering on feelings of cultural superiority. Semitic and Hamitic themes pervade Eritrean culture in subtle ways. Over the eons, Eritreans have felt that they are a special people with a historically engrained sense of endurance and perseverance under oppression. They are a people born and molded in the historical crossroads of a land that was the progenitor of civilizations. Natsnet translated this into personal strength, seeing herself as capable of great stoicism in the face of the most onerous and arduous of situations. Her experiences since leaving Eritrea, especially the scars left by her Saudi Arabian captivity, validated this.

As her life continued to demonstrate, she had a strong achievement orientation. Natsnet achieved great psychological, if not monetary, benefits from working hard, supporting her daughter and son, and doing all that she could to support her extended family still in Eritrea.

Natsnet's Faith: Much of Natsnet's life revolved around her faith. The vibrant interpretation of Orthodox tradition that she found in the Medhane Alem Movement was a key component of her life in Orange City just as it had been in all the years and troubles past. Also, the harmony, the centuries of peaceful relations found in Eritrea between Orthodox Christianity and Islamic communities transferred well to America with its pluralism and multiplicity of ethnic groups, interests, and religions. Natsnet knew that she could get along with all and not be beset by the bigotry that characterized so many of those whom she encountered in Orange City.

The Omnipresence of the Eritrean State

Even the Eritrean state was present in Natsnet's life. Forever regarded by the government as "citizens living abroad," Eritreans in the diaspora cannot escape the grip of the regime. From the regime's point of view, Eritrean citizenship cannot be renounced. Once an Eritrean, always an Eritrean, is the regime's mantra.

In every diaspora community of Eritreans, there are those who are regime loyalists, deeply committed to its values, blind to its faults, and zealous in extracting loyalty from other Eritreans. By dint of their volume, assertiveness, and ardor, they usually have impact on others whether others want to be impacted or not. No Eritrean anywhere in the world can escape the pressures placed on diaspora communities to serve the state, especially in the form of paying taxes.

One incident that terrified Natsnet stands out and it happened in her congregation in Orange City at a cleanup Saturday. When Natsnet tells it, it is obvious that she was stunned. Here is the context of the incident.

As Natsnet has shown, the Orthodox faith was of prime importance in sustaining her. In Orange City, her parish was the center of her life and the central gathering place for the few other Eritreans living in the area. In many ways, it was a much-needed cocoon for the community, a recreation of "home." This is a recurring theme of diasporic lives; wherever in the world there are newcomers to new lands, there is a yearning for what was. The church, in the person of her congregation, was also Natsnet's socio-cultural guide, interpreting a new American reality, using the categories of her past to explain the happenings of the here and now.

Even in her congregation people with whom she worshipped and socialized on a regular basis there was no consensus on the legitimacy of the current government in Asmara. Some were inflexible regime supporters, romanticizing the struggle for independence, and the sacrifices of the martyred heroes. They were loud, pushy, and zealous. Others, especially those who had left because of regime repression, were adamant in their opposition. In the middle ground were those who had fled Eritrea because of the hardships of daily life, seeming to want only to get along with their new lives in America and forget the past. When in the church, however, there was an unspoken agreement to put their political differences aside and follow an independent, middle of the road course.

Natsnet's congregation had fewer than 15 parishioners, and was served by an unpaid "worker priest," who held a full-time blue-collar job, and walked a middle ground in ministering to his congregation. The parish was not affiliated with either of the two national bodies which are split by political issues relating to the homeland. Even in the prayers, great care was taken not to cross the unspoken political line. No prayers were said for either the government deposed Eritrean patriarch, regarded by many as the legitimate leader, Antonios, or the government-installed sitting patriarch, Diascoros, seen by many as an interloper of the Eritrean government headed by Isaias. General prayers were, however, offered for the Orthodox Church and the Eritrean nation, using liturgical texts that are deeply rooted in Coptic Eritrean history, tradition, and culture. The use of *Ge'ez*, the liturgical language, had a soothing effect.

On one "cleanup Saturday" at the church, a rented storefront in a crumbling Orange City neighborhood, once a thriving place of Greek immigrants and culture, Natsnet was working on the windows, washing and polishing them to make them sparkle in the sunlight. There was a lot of friendly banter among parishioners, and as was always the case, the conversation turned to their past lives in Eritrea.

Natsnet's thoughts went to her life, growing up in Eritrea and her beloved Medhane Alem Movement a reform element, sometimes called a Sunday School Movement within the Eritrean Church. The Movement, at first accepted by the Isaias regime, was later brutally suppressed by the government as a threat to its all reaching control. Questions over its legitimacy were thoroughly intertwined with the deposition of beloved Patriarch Antonios.

One of the goals of the Medhane Alem movement "Savior of the World" in Tigrinya was the infusion of a more spirited style of worship into structured, liturgical Orthodox worship. Songs of praise were an integral part of this effort, and Natsnet, from her childhood on, had always loved these songs which reminded her of a very different way of life. She remembered the stories told of her baptism in the great cathedral and Sundays, when her family would walk together to Divine Liturgy, joining with their neighbors, singing these songs of praise. She also thought of the war for independence, of her "decision" to work in Saudi Arabia, and of her life since. The tears came; tears of happiness, sorrow, regret, and remorse. That was a very different Eritrea, and she loved and missed those times with her family so much.

Pausing from her window washing, Natsnet began to hum, then sing a favorite song of hers, "*Selam Nike,*" roughly translated as (May peace be upon on St.Mary). Her fellow congregants, now her American family, gathered around her, some joining the singing, but all embracing her and each other. Joyful words were exchanged; comments were made about the promises of the revolution, and some quite bitter words were uttered about the failures of the government, the never-ending poverty of their families still in Eritrea, and the constant government harassment. The revered Patriarch Antonios of the Eritrean Orthodox Church was deposed and held in confinement by the government in an unknown location, was frequently mentioned (Connell 2005, Mokennen and Kidane 2014).

One old man, Akhlilu (pseudo-name), a decorated veteran of the Liberation War, hung back and continued his work, seemingly oblivious to the joyful, yet in so many ways, sorrowful singing led by Natsnet. The next day, Sunday, after the social hour following Divine Liturgy, Akhlilu stopped Natsnet as she was walking with her kids to her friend's car. Brimming with emotion, he began talking and gesticulating, his voice rising from a lecturing tone to a verbal tirade, almost a fusillade:

> Natsnet: How could you have joined the others in saying those things yesterday about our government? Why are you doing this? What kind of Eritrean are you? Do you not remember the Martyrs, the suffering and the sacrifices of our people, the heroic struggle? Would you waste all of that now? We must build a new world, a new Eritrea. Are you a traitor? How can you say such things? What is wrong with you? You shouldn't be with this American and *Woyane* (referring to Ethiopian government) agents.

Even in her church in Orange City, the regime was still with her.

BACKGROUND SECTION NO.8

Eritrean State Control of Its Diaspora

In the United States, the largest concentrations of Eritreans are in several major population centers, especially the Atlanta, Baltimore-Washington, Dallas-Fort Worth, and San Francico-Oakland Bay metropolitan areas. Sizeable clusters of Eritreans are also present in the Chicago, Columbus, Denver, Indianapolis, Los Angeles, Minneapolis, Philadelphia, and San Diego areas while smaller enclaves exist elsewhere, scattered throughout the American homeland.

In general, the diaspora population is united by its patriotic feelings, selective remembrance of the homeland, and the reconstruction of homeland institutions in the diaspora. There is little consensus and a high degree of fragmentation on the political issues, particularly about the future of the Eritrean state. Degrees of support for the current regime range from the enthusiastically supportive, the passively neutral to the strongly opposed. For many Eritreans in the diaspora, the course of least resistance is simply to remain silent, tending one's own proverbial garden. This, almost by definition, gives the most vociferous and zealous a greater role than their numbers justify.

The ability of those opposed to the current regime to organize and harvest the support of the Eritrean diaspora population is hampered by the well-coordinated control mechanisms implemented by the Eritrean regime over its diaspora population (Plaut 2015, Woldu and Bromall, 2016). The foundations of the regime's control of the diaspora lies in its concept of Eritrean citizenship. From the perspective of the Eritrean party state, any person with one parent of Eritrean origin, regardless of place of birth or country of residence, is an Eritrean citizen. Citizens have duties and responsibilities to the state, no matter where in the world they live.

Working through zealots loyal to the ruling party, the Popular Front for Democracy and Justice (PFDJ), the Eritrean government coerces and intimidates the diaspora population, inducing its support, or at least its abstention from anti-regime actions (Plaut 2014, 2015 Woldu and Bromall 2016). Known as *jasus*, these agents are key contact persons middle actors in diaspora communities. They pass information about individual Eritreans' activities, especially actions and statements that suggest a questioning of the regime, to the Eritrean government through Eritrean diplomatic posts in the host country and sometimes the regime supporters could be violent (Plaut 2015, Woldu, and Bromall 2016, UN Report of the Commission of Inquiry on Human Rights in Eritrea, 2015).

The regime controls the issuance of permits to visit the homeland, rights to claim inheritance, and the securing of legal documents (e.g., birth and death certificates, property documents, etc.). Family members still living in Eritrea are often targeted for punishment for the acts of "offending" family members abroad.

Beyond expecting political loyalty, the Eritrean government also sees its diaspora population as a source of income through a two-percent tax levied on income earned abroad, special donations (e.g., to a martyrs' fund), and other levies. Such tariffs are also applied to secure state-controlled services (e.g., securing a university transcript). The Eritrean government also controls many diaspora community institutions (e.g., religious institutions, community centers, other grassroots organizations) and national community activities (e.g., Liberation Day celebrations, Martyrs' Day, etc.) (UN Report of the Commission of Inquiry on Human Rights in Eritrea, 2015, Woldu and Bromall 2016).

To build the Eritrean state's legitimacy, and solidify party control among young Eritreans, the regime organizes trips to Eritrea where sites important to the Liberation War are featured, and a major concluding festival event staged at the main military training center, Sawa. Tigrinya lessons are offered in community centers for heritage speakers. Community concerts targeted for young people are held periodically. All of these activities have, of course, a political message.

These activities and festivals are opened by visiting government officials, bringing a special message from the Eritrean president and PFDJ (the ruling party). During these events, Eritrean government representatives meet with the community and with the *jasus*. Special fund drives to collect money for homeland projects are often part of these visits (Woldu and Bromall 2016).

The Eritrean Orthodox Church is a dominant force in the life of the diaspora community. The Orthodox Church institutionalized itself in the US in 1990 with four congregations. By 2005, it had grown to 19 congregations, with 5 mission communities on the verge of establishing their own parishes. Its membership numbered about 13,500. By 2008, with the solidification of relations with the Egyptian Coptic Church, the British Orthodox Church, and other Oriental Orthodox churches, the Diocese was a significant power within the Eritrean-American community, for the most part, independent of the ruling regime.

The Eritrean government launched a major campaign to capture independent congregations in the US, sending two bishops on a whirlwind tour of parishes to rein them in to PFDJ control (Woldu and Bromall 2016). Today, the Eritrean Orthodox Church is a denomination in schism, with one wing pledging loyalty to the government and the other in opposition.

It is through tactics such as the above that the Eritrean party-state exerts control over its diaspora population (Plaut 2015).

Natsnet's Future

It would be tempting to say now that Natsnet'd legal issues are over in this "great land of opportunity," that her future is glowing and bright. This is just not the case. Natsnet has been scarred by her experiences in ways that the ordinary American cannot understand. Not only has she been sexually assaulted and physically abused, but her psyche has been damaged.

Prior to her final asylum hearing, as told in Chapter 5, Dawit and Irv had contracted with a Utah psychologist to examine her. Because of distance, limited time, and scarcity of resources, he conducted the interview with Natsnet by telephone. The psychologist was as kind and open as he could be, given the telephonic nature of the interview. Dawit was the interlocutor, translating Natsnet's answers to the psychologist. As told in Chapter 5, whatever happened, whatever was asked or said, when Irv and Dawit spoke after the interview, Dawit was deeply sad. It was an emotional conversation for all, especially for Natsnet, and it clearly touched on some very raw nerves.

Despite all of the hopeful signs that we find in Natsnet's life in Orange City, its trajectory is simply not certain. Natsent's story embodies the thousands of women trafficked, abused, and exploited every day in the most inhuman way. Experiences that of Natsent and many others challenge our collective humanistic values and calls on us to make the world a better place for those whose voices, bodies and minds have been oppressed in the most fundamental ways.

CHAPTER 12. CONCLUSIONS

Our work does not provide easy answers to immigration and human trafficking problems millions of people are experiencing every month. We are not advocating political problems and human rights violation at home are the only reasons why people migrate or fall victims of human trafficking. However, our work attempts to provide political and social pathways to immigration and human trafficking in the Middle East and sub-Saharan Africa. Our work also emphasizes the socio-cultural, economic and health challenges immigrants face in the United States to lead a normal life and the price tag associated to get immigration status and justice. The main goal of our work is to highlights the political and at times social forces, and economic factors that push women to seek employment as immigrants in immigrants' unfriendly Gulf countries. This book outlines the main structural mechanisms to the production of migration such as abject poverty, uninformed decisions, getting tricked by traffickers and recruiting companies, and repressive and corrupt governments at home. Some of the women that seek employment in Saudi Arabia kingdom and other Gulf countries are actually educated and professionals but could not find a job in their countries or the salary is very minimal. Therefore, Natsnet is not alone in this and there are so many other women from different backgrounds who became victims of domestic servitude in Saudi Arabia and other oil rich countries in the region. According to (Anti-Slavery international 2006) there are close to 4 million domestic workers in Saudi Arabia, the largest being from Philippines (about a million), Indonesia, India, Yemen, and Ethiopia. Most of these women generally face similar treatment and are subjected to persistent exploitation. In addition to the different forms of exploitation harassment there are some anecdotal reports and YouTube posts that show cases of women being beaten to death or thrown from high apartment buildings in some Middle Eastern countries.

Examples of these violence and exploitation of women in Saudi Arabia have been presented by several NGOs and governments including the United States annual human right report, amnesty international etc. For example, a story compiled by postivenegatives.org, an NGO working on violence against women in many parts of the world provides the details of how domestic workers industry works in Saudi Arabia. The story is presented in a comic book format about the journey of an Ethiopian women named Almaz (pseudo name) from her country to Saudi Arabia, her life in Saudi Arabia, and the final outcome of her domestic servitude in Saudi Arabia and the story can be accessed in the BBC website at http://www.bbc.com/news/magazine-29415876. It is quite a tragic story that sheds light to the story we documented in the previous chapters about Natsent. They both share the same experience in Saudi Arabia but finally with different outcome.

Nastnet story is not just a particular story, it is a story shared by millions of women who are kept behind doors in Saudi Arabia's domestic workers' industry and are subjected to unfortunate physical and mental repression on a daily basis. Nastnet and Almaz share similar story both from a cultural and captivity experience. The circumstances coming to Saudi Arabia might be different but the underlying cause to their overall problem is the same basic lack of economic opportunity at home or political repression as in the case of Natsent. However, once in Saudi Arabia, they both were mobbing the floors of rich Saudi Arabian families, they were sexually harassed by men, they were assaulted and insulted by their Saudi Arabian women masters. Above all, they were prisoners of a system that does not see female maid workers as equals who deserve a dignified life. Natsent was lucky to escape the horror she faced in Saudi Arabia and finally coming to the US and eventually winning her freedom. However, Almaz faced a different fate, a fate that defined her life forever, a woman with disability and all the social stigmas that comes with it. It is a very touching story that aches the heart and mind of any sensible human being. Almaz and Natsnet define and embody the resilience of our humanity and the strength and story of two women who provide us a plenty of opportunity to change the course of history and shape the future of our children and the equality of men and women in our globe. We hope there is a brighter future for Almaz and Natsent and many others victims of inequality, injustice, violence and oppression. Finally, we hope their story evokes and brings the brighter side of our humanity.

BIBLIOGRAPHY

Abraha, D. "Command Economy as failed model of development: Lessons not yet learned: The case of Eritrea." *Journal of Management Policy and Practice* Vol.11 No. 5 (2010):49-68

ACCORD News: "Unravelling HIV/AIDS related Stigma." Issue #3 (2014). http://www.acordinternational.org/silo/files/unravelling-hiv-and-aids-related-stigma.pdf

Adam, Liptak. "Witness Feels Betrayed as U.S. Plans to Divide Family." *New York Times*. 8 August 2011.

Afifi, Tamer. "Economic or Environmental Migration? The Push factor in Niger." *International Migration*, Vol. 49, Issue supplement S1 (2011): e96-e124.doi:10.1111/j.1468-2435.2010.00644.x

Akinola, Olufemi. "Politics and Identity Construction in Eritrean Studies, c. 1970-1991: The Making of Voix Érythrée." *African Study Monographs*, Vol. 28, No. 2, (2007). 47-86

Alexander III, B, Sydeham. "A Political Response to Crisis in the Immigration Courts." *Georgetown Immigration Law Journal*, Vol. 21, No. 2 (2006)

Ali, H. Ayanan. *Infidel*. New York: Free Press, 2008.

American Bar Association, Commission on Immigration. *Reforming the Immigration System: Proposals to Promote, Independence,*

Fairness, Efficiency, and Professionalism in the Adjudication f Removal Cases. Washington, DC: ABA, 2010.

Amnesty International. "Document - Libya: 200 Eritreans in Libya at risk of forced return," 2 July 2010.http://www.amnesty.org/en/library/info/MDE19/015/2010/en

Amnesty International. "Document - Libya: Eritrean nationals released in Libya," 7 September 2010.http://www.amnesty.org/en/library/info/MDE19/018/2010/en

Amnesty International. *Amnesty International Report 2010: The State of the World's Human Rights,* "Eritrea," 2010.

Amnesty International. "Eritrea: 20 years of Independence, but still no freedom." May 2013. http://www.amnesty.org/en/library/asset/AFR64/001/2013/en/64b58cdf-a431-499c-9830-f4d66542c8da/afr640012013en.pdf.

Anti-Slavery International 2006 Report: "Trafficking in women: Forced labor and Domestic work in the Context of Middle East and Gulf Region"

Armstrong, A.G. *History of Eritrea*. Amazon.com: Kindle eBook, 2012.

Asgedom, Mawi. *Of Beetles and Angels: A Boy's Remarkable Journey from a Refugee Camp to Harvard*. New York: Little Brown Books for Young Readers, 2002.

Ashine, Argaw. "How does 'poor' Eritrea afford to fund Al-Shabaab?" *The Citizen*. 9 November 2011. http://thecitizen.co.tz/editorial-analysis/20-analysis-opinions/16938-how-does-poor-eritrea-afford-to-fund-al-shabaab.html.

Augustana Heritage Association. http://augustanaheritage.org/index.php. Accessed 29 January 2012.

Barley, Nigel. *The Innocent Anthropologist: Notes from a Mud Hut*. Long Grove, IL: Waveland Press, Inc., 1983 (reissued 2000).

Bell, Steward. "Eritreans pressured to pay 'diaspora tax' to Eritrean diplomats and agents in Canada to finance terrorist groups to attack us." *CIReport*. http://www.cireport.ca/tag/eritrean-diplomats. 23 March 2012.)

Bell, Stuart. "Eritrea raising money in Canada, financing terrorists to attack Canada." *National Post*." 5 November 2011.

http://news.nationalpost.com/2011/11/05/eritrea-is-raising-money-in-canada-and-financing-terrorists-that-want-to-attack-canada/.

Bellos. David. *Is That a Fish in Your Ear?: Translation and the Meaning of Everything*. New York: Faber & Faber, 2011.

Bereketeab, Redie. "The Eritrean Diaspora: Myth and Reality" in Ulf Johansson Dahre, editor. The Role of Diasporas in Peace, Democracy and Development in the Horn of Africa. Lund, Sweden: Social Anthropology, Department of Sociology, and Department of Political Science; Lund University & Somalia International Rehabilitation Center. Research Report in Social Anthropology, (Printed by Media-Tryck Sociologen, Lunds universitet), (2007):79-96.

Bernal, Victoria. "Diaspora, cyberspace and political imagination: The Eritrean diaspora online." *Global Networks*, Vol. 6, Issue 2, (2006):161-179.

Bernal, Victoria. "Eritrea and the Global Village: Reflections on Nationalism in Transnational Era." *Cultural Anthropology* Vol.19 No2. (2004):1-25

Bernard, R._*Social Science Research Methods*: Qualitative and *Quantitative approaches*, 4th edition. Sage Publications, Thousand Oaks, California, USA, 2013.

Betsy Adeboyejo, American Bar Association News Service. "ABA Advocates Solutions to Overburdened Immigration Court System: Association calls for more resources to handle record immigration enforcement efforts." 19 May 2011. Accessed 26 November 2011.

Beydoun, A., Khaled. "The Trafficking of Ethiopian Domestic Workers into Lebanon: Navigating Through a Newel Passage of the International Maid Trade." *Berkeley Journal of International Law*. Vol. 24, No. 3 (2006):250-286.

Biehl, João & Peter Locke. "Deluze and the Anthropology of Becoming." Current Anthropology, Vol. 51, No. 3 (2010): 317-351.

Bowen, Elenor. *Return to Laughter: An Anthropological Novel*. [Place]: Doubleday, Anchor, 1964.

Bozzini, M., David. "Low-tech Surveillance and the Despotic State in Eritrea." *Surveillance & Society*, Vol 9, No. ½, (2011): 93-113.

Brettell, C.B. and Hollifield, J.F. (Eds.). *Migration Theory: Talking Across Disciplines*. Third Edition. Routledge, Oxford UK, 2014.

Brhane, M.O 'Trafficking in Persons for Ransom and the Need to Expand the Interpretation of Article 3 of the UN Trafficking Protocol. *Anti-Trafficking Review*, issue 4, (2015):120—141, www.antitraffickingreview.org

Brown, W. Garrett & David Held, eds., *The Cosmopolitan Reader*. Cambridge, England, UK & Malden, MA: Polity Press, 2011.

Cannuyer. Christian. *Coptic Egypt: The Christians of the Nile*. New York: Harry N. Abrams, Inc., 2001.

Carol Sanders. "Eritreans in Canada shaken down by despot back home." *Winnepeg Free Press*. 25 November 2011. Accessed 27 November 2011.

Chait, M., Sandra. *Seeking Salaam: Ethiopian, Eritreans, and Somalis in the Pacific Northwest*. Seattle: University of Washington Press, 2011.

Cheah, Pheng & Bruce Robbins, eds., *Cosmopolitics: Thinking and Feeling Beyond the Nation*. Minneapolis: University of Minnesota Press, 1998.

Chua, Amy. World on Fire: How Exporting Free Market Democracy Breeds Ethnic Hatred and Global Instability. New York: Anchor, 2004.

Connell, Dan & Tom Killion. *Historical Dictionary of Eritrea*, 2nd ed. Lanham, MD, Toronto, & Plymouth, UK: Scarecrow Press, 2010.

Connell, Dan. "Eritrea." *Conflict Analysis*, Vol. 2, No. 45, (1997).

Connell, Dan. *Against All Odds: A Chronicle of the Eritrean Revolution*. Lawrenceville, NJ & Asmara, Eritrea: Red Sea Press, Inc., 1993 & 1997.

Connell, Dan. *Conversations with Eritrean Political Prisoners*. Lawrenceville, NJ & Asmara, Eritrea: Red Sea Press, Inc., 2005.

Connell, Dan. *Taking on the Superpowers: Collected Articles on the Eritrean Revolution, 1976-1982.* Lawrenceville, NJ & Asmara, Eritrea: Red Sea Press, Inc., 2003.

Conrad, Bettina. "'Out of the 'Memory Hole': Alternative Narratives of the Eritrean Revolution in the Diaspora. *Afrika Spectrum,* Vol. 41, No. 2, (2006): 249-271

Conrad, Bettina. "'We Are the Warsay of Eritrea in Diaspora': Contested Identities and Social Divisions in Cyberspace" in Leif Manger and Manzoul A.A. Assal, eds. *Diasporas within and without Africa.* Uppsala: Nordiska Afrikainstitutet, 2006.

Conrad, Bettina. "From Revolution to Religion: The Politics of Religion in the Eritrean Diaspora in Germany." In Afe Adogame und Cordula Welsskӧppel, eds, *Religion in the Context of African Migration Studies.* Bayreuth African Studies Series 75, (2005): 217-241.

Conrad, Bettina. "When a Culture of War Meets a Culture of Exile: Second Generation Diaspora Eritreans and their Relations to Eritrea: *Revue Européene des Migrations Internationales,* Vol. 22, No.1, (2006): 59-85.

Conrad, Bettina. "When Neverland Meets Otherland: Virtual Communities and Real-Life Divisions in the Eritrean Diaspora." In Siegbert Uhlig. Proceedings of the XVth International Conference on Ethiopian Studies. Hamburg, (2003): 58-65.

Conrad, Bettina. "'We Are the Prisoners of Our Dreams': Exit, Voice, and Loyality in the Eritrean Diaspora in Germany." *Eritrean Studies Review,* Vol. 4, No. 2, (2005): 211-261.doi:10.1017/S0022278X05001059

Dahre, Ulf Johansson, editor., *"The Role of Diasporas in Peace, Democracy and Development in the Horn of Africa."* Lund, Sweden: Social Anthropology, Department of Sociology, and Department of Political Science; Lund University & Somalia International Rehabilitation Center. Research Report in Social Anthropology, (Printed by Media-Tryck Sociologen, Lunds universitet), 2007.

Denison, Edward & Edward Paice. *Eritrea: The Brandt Travel Guide*, 4th ed. Bucks, England, UK & Guilford, CT: The Globe Pequot Press, 2007.

DeParle, Jason. "The Anti-Immigration Crusader." *New York Times*. 17 April 2011.

Deutscher, Guy. *Through the Language Glass: Why the World Looks Different in Other Languages*. Metropolitan Books, 2010/

DeWalt M, and Billie DeWalt. *Participant observation: A guide for field workers.* Altamira Press, Eastover Road, Playmouth, United Kingdom, 2011.

DHS to conduct case-by-case review on deportation. CNN.com. Accessed 18 August 2011.

Dolnick, Sam. "Immigrants May Be Fed False Stories to Bolster Asylum Pleas." *New York Times*. 11 July 2011.

Domestic worker abuse. CNN.com, 15 November 2011.

Dooling, Richard. *White Man's Grave*. New York: Farrar, Straus and Giroux. 1994.

Dorman, S. "Narratives of Nationalism in Eritrea: Research and Revisionism." *Nations and Nationalism*, 11 No.2 (2005):203-222

Doumato, A. Eleanor. Gender, Monarchy and National Identity in Saudi Arabia. *British Journal of Middle Eastern Studies*, Vol.19. No.1, (1992):31-47

Dutchmen grounded. *The Economist*. 7 January 2012. Pages 51-52.

Ehrenreich, Barbara & Arlie Russell Hothschild, eds. "*Global Woman: Nannies, Maids, and Sex Workers in the New Economy*." New York: Metropolitan Books, 2003.

Emerson, M. Robert, Fretz, Rachel I., Shaw, Linda L. *Writing Ethnographic Fieldnotes*. Chicago: University of Chicago Press, 1995.

"Eritrea and Its Unusual Embassies." Gedeb News. 21 October 2010. http://awate.com/eritrea-and-its-unusual-embassies-2/

"Eritrean Diaspora Money and Al Shabaab." Asmarino Editorial. 26 March 2010. http://asmarino.com/articles/615-eritrean-diaspora-money-and-al-shabaab.

Eritrean Movement for Democracy and Human Rights – EMDHR. "Eritrea: Youth and Militarisation." A discussion paper presented to the European Union Delegation, Meron Estefanos, presenter, 1 July 2008, Brussels, Belgium.

Eyassu, Nebiyu. *"Ethiopian Exile: A microcosm of African Diaspora."* Amazon.com: self-published by Nebiyu Eyassu, 2013.

Faddiman, Anne. *The Spirit Catches You and You Fall Down*. New York: Farrar, Straus and Giroux. 1998.

Farmer, Paul. *Pathologies of Power: Health, Human Rights, and the New War on the Poor*. Berkeley: University of California Press, 2004.

Feingold, A. David. "Human Trafficking." *Foreign Policy*. No. 150 (2005):26-30, 32.

Fernandez, Bina. *Transformative Policy for Poor Women*. UK, Ashgate, 2012.

Forced Migration Online. http://www.forcedmigration.org/about, August 2015

Freedom House. "Eritrea," in "Freedom in the World" (2010). http://www.freedomhouse.org/template.cfm?page=22&country=7819&year=2010

Freedom House. "Freedom in the World – Eritrea" (2010). http://www.freedomhouse.org/template.cfm?page=363&year=2010

Gale Reference Team. "U.S. Asylum System: Significant Variation Existed in Asylum Outcomes across Immigrations Courts and Judges. Stonehedge: General Accounting Office Reports & Testimony, 1 November 2008.

Gebremedhin, Tesfa. *Women, tradition, and development in Africa: the Eritrean case*. Lawrenceville, NJ: Red Sea Press, 2001

Genet, Kumera. "Maid in Lebanon: Ethiopian and Lebanese Reactions to the Death of Alem, and Slavery in Lebanon." Posted 13 April 2012; get updates from Khaled A.Beydoun. Appearing in *Huffington Post*. 19 April 2012.

Genzuk, Michael. A Synthesis of Ethnographic Research. Occasional Papers Series. Center for Multilingual, Multicultural Research (Eds.). Center for Multilingual, Multicultural Research, Rossier School of Education, University of Southern California. Los Angeles, 2003.

Getahun, Solomon, *The History of Ethiopian Immigrants and Refugees in America, 1900-2000: Patterns of Migration, Survival, and Adjustment*. New York: LFB Scholarly Publishing, 2007.

Gibrael, Mikeal, Archdeacon Habeeb Guirguis (translated into English by Shaeer Gobran) (Sidney: Sunday School Central Committee [of the Coptic Orthodox Church {Egypt}], 1991). Note: This was taken from the diocesan website of Eritrean Orthodox Church in North America and subtitled Spiritual Food: The Renaissance of Coptic Orthodox Church after long years of darkness and is commended the Eritrean Orthodox Church as "A Role Model for the Eritrean Orthodox Church." It is thus an appropriate information source on the Medhane Alem movement in today's Eritrean Orthodox Church.

Global Migration Group. *"International Migration and Human Rights: Challenges and opportunities on the threshold of the 60th Anniversary of the universal declaration of human rights."* 2008 http://www.unhcr.org/cgibin/texis/vtx/home/opendocPDFViewer.html?docid=49e479cf0&query=Key%20terms

Gordon, Frances & Jean-Bernard Carillet. *Ethiopia & Eritrea*, 2nd ed. NP: Lonely Planet Publications, 2003.

Gunn, W and Louis Logstrup : "Participant observation, anthropology methodology and design anthropology research inquiry." *Journal of Arts and Humanities in higher education*, Vol.13 No. 4 (2014): 428-442.

Habte Selassie, Bereket. *The Crown and The Pen: The Memoirs of a Lawyer Turned Rebel*. Lawrenceville, NJ, & Asmara: Red Sea Press, 2007.

Habtom, J.W. *Lonely Without Me: A Memoir: My journey across five continents in search of home*. Hyab Publishers, 2011.

Halabi, Rominis "Contract Enslavement of Female Migrant Domestic Workers in Saudi Arabia and the United Arab Emirates,"

Human Rights & Human Welfare, May 2008 (published online by the Graduate School of International Studies, University of Denver).

Halliday, Fred. *Nation and Religion in the Middle East*. Lynne Renner Publishers, Boulder, Colorado, USA, 2000.

Held, David. "Principles of Cosmopolitan Order," in Garrett Wallace Brown & David Held, eds., *The Cosmopolitan Reader*. Cambridge, England, UK & Malden, MA: Polity Press, (2011): 229-247.

Henze. Paul. Layers of time: *A History of Ethiopia*. New York: Palgrave, 2000.

Hepner, R., Tricia. "Seeking asylum, autonomy, and human rights: Eritreans in Germany and the United States. Paper presented to the School of African Studies (University of London) conference. 16 April 2009.

Hepner, R., Tricia. "Eritrean Immigrants." In Ron Bayor, ed., *Encyclopedia of Multicultural America*. Westport, CT: Greenwood Publishing, Vol.2 (2011): 617-655

Hepner, Tricia "Seeking Asylum in a Transnational Social Field." David O'Kane & Tricia Redeker Hepner, eds. *Biopolitics, Militarism, and Development*: Eritrea in the Twenty-First Century. New York & Oxford, UK: Berghahn Books, (2011):115-133.

Hepner. Tricia. *Soldiers, Martyrs, Traitors, and Exiles: Political Conflict in Eritrea and the Diaspora (The Ethnography of Political Violence.)* Philadelphia: University of Pennsylvania Press, 2011.

Hill, Justin. Cio Asmara: *A Classic Account of Contemporary Africa*. London: Little, Brown Book Group, 2004.

Human Rights Watch, "Service for Life: State Repression and Indefinite Conscription in Eritrea," 16 April 2009. http://www.hrw.org/en/reports/2009/04/15/service-life-0

Human Rights Watch, *World Report 2010,* 20 January 2010.http://www.hrw.org/en/reports/2010/01/20/world-report-2010

Huus, Kari. "American seeks political asylum in Sweden, alleging torture, FBI coercion." Msnbc.com, 19 April 2012.

Ibrahim Foundation, *The Ibrahim Index*, 2007-2010, 4 October 2010. http://www.moibrahimfoundation.org/en

"In praise of a second (or third) passport." *The Economist*. 7 January 2012. Page 12.

International Crisis Group, "Eritrea: The Siege State," 21 September 2010.

International Labour Organization in collaboration with the Ministry of Labour and Social Affairs, the Ethiopian Employers' Federation, and the Confederation of Ethiopian Trade Unions. *Trafficking in Persons Overseas for Labour Purposes: The Case of Ethiopian Domestic Workers*." Addis Ababa: ILO Country Office Addis Ababa, 2011.

International Labour Organization. Simel Esim & Monica Smith, eds. *Gender and Migration in Arab States: The Case of Domestic Workers." Trafficking in Persons Overseas for Labour Purposes: The Case of Ethiopian Domestic Workers*." Beirut: Regional Office for Arab States, June 2004.

Irvin H. Bromall. "Lawyers in Politics: An Exploratory Study of the Wisconsin Bar." *Wisconsin Law Review* 751, (1968).

Iyob, Ruth. "The Ethiopian-Eritrean conflict: diasporic vs. hegemonic states in the Horn of Africa, 1991-2000." *The Journal of Modern African Studies*, Vol. 28, No. 4, (2000): 559-682.

Iyob, Ruth. *The Eritrean Struggle for Independence: Domination, Resistance, Natoinalism, 1941-1993*. New York: Cambridge University Press, 1997.

Jenkins, Craig. "Pull/Push in recent Mexican migrations to the US." *International Migration Review Volume* 11, No. 2, (1977): 178-189.

Jenkins, Philip. The New Faces of Christianity: Believing the Bible in the Global South. Oxford & New York: Oxford University Press, 2006.

Johnson, JC, Christine Avenarius, and Jack Weatherford. Active participant-observer: "Applying social role analysis to participant observation." *Field Methods*, Vol. 18 No.2 (2006):111-134.

Kälin, Walter. "Troubled Communication: Cross-Cultural Misunderstanding in the Asylum-Hearing." *International Migration Review*. Vol. 20, No. 2, Special Issue: (1986):230-241.

Kaufman, Herbert. The Forest Ranger: *A Study in Administrative Behavior*. Washington, DC: Rff Press, 2006. (Originally published 1960.)

Kearny, Edward, Mary Ann Kearny, and Jo Ann Crandall. *The American Way: An Introduction to American Culture*. Englewood Cliffs, NJ: Prentice Hall, 1984.

Kendie, Daniel. *The Five Dimensions of the Eritrean Conflict: 1941 – 2004*. N.p.: Signature Book Publishing, Inc., 2005.

Keneally, Thomas. *To Asmara. Boston*: Grand Central Publishing, 1990.

Kenney, David & Philip G. Schrag. Asylum Denied: *A Refugee's Struggle for Safety in America*. Berkeley & Los Angeles: University of California Press, 2009

Kibreab, Gaim. "Forced labour in Eritrea." *Journal of Modern African Studies*, Vol. 47, No. 1 (2009): 41-72.

Kibreab, Gaim. "The Eritrean Diaspora, the War of Independence, Post-Conflict (Re)-construction and Democratisation" in Ulf Johansson Dahre, editor. *The Role of Diasporas in Peace, Democracy and Development in the Horn of Africa*. Lund, Sweden: Social Anthropology, Department of Sociology, and Department of Political Science; Lund University & Somalia International Rehabilitation Center. Research Report in Social Anthropology, (Printed by Media-Tryck Sociologen, Lunds universitet), (2007): 87-115.

Kibreab, Gaim. *Refugees and Development in Africa: The Case of Eritrea*. Lawrenceville, NJ & Asmara, Eritrea: Red Sea Press, Inc., 1987.

Kibreab, Gaim. Eritrea: *A Dream Deferred*. Oxford: James Currey and Uppsala: Nordiska Afrikainstitutet, (2009): xxvi-420

Kleinman, Arthur. *Patients and Healers in the Context of Culture: An Exploration of the Borderland Between Anthropology, Medicine, and Psychiatry*. Berkeley: University of California Press, 1981.

Koser, Khalid, editor. *New African Diasporas (Global Diaspora)*, especially Chapter 7, "Mobilizing New African Diasporas: An Eritrean Case Study." London & New York: Routledge, 2003.

Krieble Foundation. *The Red Card Solution: Bringing Order to US Borders*. November 2010 white paper

Krikorian. Mark. *The New Case Against Immigration: Both Legal and Illegal*. New York: Sentinel (Penguin Group [USA]), 2008.

Kymlicka, Will, "Citizenship in an Era of Globalization," in Garrett Wallace Brown & David Held, eds., *The Cosmopolitan Reader*. Cambridge, England, UK & Malden, MA: Polity Press, (2011): 435-443.

Lata, Leenco. *Peacekeeping as State Building: Current Challenges for the Horn of Africa*. Lawrenceville, NJ, & Asmara: Red Sea Press, 2011.

Lessinger, Johanna. *From Ganges to Hudson: Indian immigrants in New York City*. New York: Allyn and Bacon Press, 1995.

Lewis, Bernard. *Race and Slavery in the Middle East: An Historical Enquiry*. New York: Oxford University Press. 1992.

Linarelli, John. "Violence against Women and the Asylum Process." *60 Albany Law Review* 977 (1996-1997):977.

Long, David. *Culture and Customs of Saudi Arabia*. Green wood Press, West port, Connecticut, USA, 2005.

Lossky, Vladimir. *The Mystical Theology of the Eastern Church*. Crestwood, NY: St. Vladimir's Seminary Press, 1976.

Lustig, L. Stuart, Kevin Delucchi, Lakshika Tennadoon, Brent Kaul, Hon. Dana Leigh Marks, Hhon, and Denise Slavin . "Burnout and Stress Among United States Immigration Judges. 13 Bender's Immigration Bulletin, 2008.

Maisel, Sebastian and John Shoup. *Saudi Arabia and The Gulf Arab States Today: An Encyclopedia of life in the Arab States*. Green Wood Press, Connecticut, USA 2009.

Mamdani, Mahmood. "Political Identity, Citizenship and Ethnicity in Post-Colonial Africa." Keynote Address, Arusha Conference, "New Frontiers of Social Policy," 12-15 December 2005. Draft working paper produced for the World Bank conference, "New Frontiers of Social Policy: Development in a Globalizing World." http://siteresources.worldbank.org/INTRANETSOCIALDEVELOPMENT/Resources/revisedMamdani.pdf

Manby, Bronwen. *Citizenship Law in Africa: A Comparative Study*. New York: Open Society Foundations, Africa Governance Monitoring and Advocacy Project (AfriMAP), Open Society Justice Initiative, 2010

Margolis, Maxine. Little Brazil: *An ethnography of Brazilian Immigrants in New York City*. New Jersey: Princeton University Press, 1994.

Martin,C. Daniels and James E. Yankay. Refugees and Asylees: 2013. Annual Flow Report, August 2014. http://www.dhs.gov/sites/default/files/publications/ois_rfa_fr_2013.pdf

Mattar, Y., Mohamed. "Trafficking in Persons, Especially Women and Children, in Countries of the Middle East: The Scope of the Problem and Appropriate Legislative Responses." *Fordham International Law Journal*. Vol. 26, Issue 3 (2002):721-760.

Mauri, Arnaldo. "Eritrea's early stages in monetary and banking development." Working Paper, 28 October 2003. Dipartimento di Economia Politica e Aziendale, Università degli Studi di Milano, Milano, Italia.

Mayorkas, Alejandro (Director, U.S. Citizenship and Immigration Services, Department of Homeland Security). "Ensuring the Integrity of the U.S. Immigration System." In Washington, DC, IBM Center for The Business of Government, The Business of Government. Spring/Summer (2011): 27-29.

McGovern, Mike. "Before You Judge, Stand in Her Shoes." *New York Times*. 5 July 2011. Accessed 6 July 2011.

Mediterranean a cemetery, Maltese Prime minter: *BBC*. 12 October 2013. http://www.bbc.com/news/world-europe-24502279

Mehret Ghebreyesus. "Eritrean Political and Human Rights Crisis– The U.S. Perspective." Europe External Policy Advisors, Eritrean Briefing Documents, No. 2. 3 March 2008.

Mekonnen, Daniel R and Kidane, Selam. "The troubled relationship of state and religion in Eritrea." *African Human Rights Law Journal*, Vol.11, No.1, (2011):244 265

Mekonnen, Daniel Rezene and Estefanos, Meron, From Sawa to the Sinai Desert: The Eritrean Tragedy of Human Trafficking (November 30, 2011). Available at SSRN: http://ssrn.com/abstract=2055303 or http://dx.doi.org/10.2139/ssrn.20553

Mekonnen, R., Daniel. "Pre- and Post-Migration Patterns of Victimisation among Eritrean Refugees in the Netherlands." Paper given at the panel, Eritrea – A Country Losing Its People, on 18 June 2011, at the Fourth European Conference on African Studies, The Nordic Africa Institute, Uppsala, Sweden, 15-18 June 2011.

Mengistu, Dinaw. *The Beautiful Things That Heaven Bears*. New York: Riverhead Books, 2007.

Mertz, Elizabeth. The Language of Law School: Learning to "Think Like a Lawyer". New York: Oxford University Press, 2007.

Moaddel, Mansoor. "The Saudi Public Speakes: Religion, Gender, and Politics." *International Journal of Middle East Studies*, 38, (2006): 79-108. doi:10.1017/S0020743806412265.

Molho, Ian. "Theories of Migration. A Review" *Scottish Journal of Political Economy*, Vol.60 No. 5 (1986): 526-553.

Mowbray, Joel. "Maids, Slaves and prisoners: To be employed in a Saudi Home." *National Review* vol.55, No.3 (2003).

"National service: miserable and useless." *The Economist*, 10 March 2014.

Negash, Tekeste and Kjetil Tronvoll (contributor). *Brothers at War: Making Sense of the Eritrean-Ethiopian War.* Athens, OH: Ohio University Press, 2001.

Negash, Tekeste. *Eritrea and Ethiopia: The Federal Experience*. Transaction Publishers, 1997.

Negash, Tekeste. *Eritrea and Ethiopia: The Federal Experience*. Uppsala, Sweden: Nordic Africa Institute, 1997.

Nicole, Hirt and Abdulkader Saleh Mohammad. "Dreams don't come true in Eritrea': anomie and family disintegration due to the structural militarisation of society." *The Journal of*

Modern African Studies, 51, (2003):139-168. doi:10.1017/S0022278X12000572.

Nur, Salih. "Foreign Policy of Eritrea: Explained in the light of "democratic peace" proposition." *International Journal of Peace and Development Studies*, Vol. No.4 (2013):76-89. DOI: 10.5897/IJPDS2013.0178

O'Kane, David & Tricia Redeker Hepner, eds. *Biopolitics, Militarism, and Development*: Eritrea in the Twenty-First Century. New York & Oxford, UK: Berghahn Books, 2011.

OCP, "The Detained Patriarch, Persecuted Christians and a Dying Church." 18 January 2012.http://theorthodox-church.info/blog/news/2012/01/the-detained-patriarch-persecuted-christians-and-a-dying-church/.

Ottaway, Marina & David. *Ethiopia: Empire in Revolution*. New York & London: African Publishing Company, 1978.

Pantucci, Raffaello. "Al-Shabaab Proscribed in Canada and the United Kingdom." *Terrorism Monitor*. Volume 8, Issue 11. 19 March 2010.

Patt, Martin, Professor Emeritus, University of Massachusetts. *Human Trafficking & Modern-day Slavery – Saudi Arabia*. http.gvnet.com/humantrafficking/SaudiArabia.htlm.

Patt, Martin. Professor Emeritus, University of Massachusetts. *Human Trafficking & Modern-day Slavery – United Arab Emirates (UAE)*.http.gvnet.com/humantrafficking/UnitedArabEmirates.htlm. 5 August 2011.

Pear, Robert. "Fewer Youths to Be Deported in New Policy." *New York Times*. 18 August 2011.

Plaut, Martin. Eritrea Sinster-international-network of spies and thugs. 04 September 2015. http://www.harnnet.org/index.php/articles-corner/english-articles/item/1962-eritrea-s-sinister-international-network-of-spies-and-thugs

Plaut, Martin. Eritrea: How the London Embassy from forces Eritreans to pay the illegal 2% tax. 16 of February 2014. https://martinplaut.wordpress.com/2014/02/16/eritrea-how-the-london-embassy-forces-eritreans-to-pay-the-illegal-2-tax-full-report/

Pogge, T. "World Poverty and Human Rights. Ethics & International Affairs, post-war nation-state." *The Journal of Modern African Studies*, 43, (2005): 467-488

Preston, Julia. "A Family Reunited After a Rare Return from Deportation." *New York Times*. 7 August 2011.

Ramji-Nogales, Jaya, Andrew Schoenholtz, Philip Schrag, & Edward Kennedy. *Refugee Roulette: Disparities in Asylum Adjudication and Proposals for Reform*. New York: New York University Press, 2011.

Reid, R. "Caught in the headlights of history: Eritrea, the EPLF and the post war nation state." *The Journal of Modern African Studies*, Vol.43, No.03 (2005):467 - 488. DOI: 10.1017/S0022278X05001059

Reid, Richard. *Frontiers of Violence in North-East Africa: Genealogies of Conflict since c. 1800*. New York: Oxford University Press, 2011.

Reisen, MV and Rijken, C. "Sinai Trafficking: Origin and Definition of a New Form of Human Trafficking." *Social Inclusion* Vol. 3, Issue 1, (2015):113-124 Doi: 10.17645/si.v3i1.180

Revelations. "Engaging the Eritrean Diaspora: Wikileaks." *Ethiopian Review*. 30 June 2011. http://www.ethiopianreview.com/forum/viewtopic.php?f=2&t=29059.

Riggan, Jennifer. "In Between Nations: Ethiopian-Born Eritreans, Liminality, and War." *PoLAR: Political and Legal Anthropology Review*, Vol. 34, No.1, (2011): 131-154.

Roper, D. Steven and Lilian Barria. Eastern Illinois University. "Labor Migration to the Gulf: Understanding Variations in the Kafala System." *Middle East Law and Governance Journal*, 6 (2014):32-52

Rosenblum, Marc and Idean Salehyan. "Norms and Interest in US Asylum Enforcement." *Journal of Peace Research* Vol.4, No.6, (2004):677-697

Salvadore, Matteo. "The Ethiopian Age of Exploration: Prester John's Discovery of Europe, 1306-1458. *Journal of World History*, Vol. 21, Issue 4, (2010):593-628.

Salvadore, Matteo. "The Jesuit mission to Ethiopia (1555-1634) and the death of Prester John. In Alllison B. Kavey, ed. *World-Building and the Early Modern Imagination*. New York: Palgrave Macmillan, (2010):141-172.

Schiller, Nina Glick, Linda Basch, & Cristina Szanton Blanc. "From Immigrant to Transmigrant: Theorizing Transnational Migration." *Anthropological Quarterly*, Vol. 68, No.1 (1995):48-63.

Schmitz-Pranghe, Clara. "Modes and Potential of Diaspora Engagement in Eritrea. DIASPEACE Working Paper No. 3, July 2010.

Semple, Kirk. "Immigrant Detentions Draw International Fire." *New York Times*. 17 March 2011.

Seraphim, Abba. *How shall we sing a new song in a strange land?* London: British Orthodox Press, 2010. (Address at the 12th Annual Assembly of the Eritrean Orthodox Diocese of North America, Stamford, CT, 24 July 2010.

Shaffer, E. et al. "Global trade and public health." *American Journal of Public Health*, Vol 95 No.1 (2005): 23-34.

Singer, M. Drugging the poor: Legal and illegal Drug industries and the structuring of social inequalities. Long Grove, IL: Waveland Press, 2008

Sishangne, Shumet. *Unionists and Separatists: The Vagaries of Ethio-Eritrean Relation – 1941 – 1991*. Hollywood, CA: Tsehai Publishers, 2007.

Slavin, Denise Noonan and Dana Leigh Marks. "Conflicting Roles of Immigration Judges: Do You Want Your Case Heard by a 'Government Attorney' or by a 'Judge'?" *Bender's Immigration Bulletin*, Vol. 16, (2011):1785-92.

Storti, Craig. *The Art of Crossing Cultures*, 2nd ed. Yarmouth, ME: Intercultural Press, (first published by Intercultural Press, 1989), 2001.

Stuart Munro-Hay. *Ethiopia, The Unknown Land: A Cultural and Historical Guide*. London & New York: I.B. Tauris Publishers, 2002.

Swain, Carol eds. *Debating Immigration*. New York: Cambridge University Press, 2007.

Tareke, Gebru. *The Ethiopian Revolution: War in the Horn of Africa*. New Haven & London: Yale University Press, 2009.

Taussing, M. Shamanism. *Colonialism and the wild man: A study in Terror and Healing*. Chicago University press, 1987.

Tezare, Kizanet, Tsehay Said, Dr. Daniel Bahets, Helen W. Tewolder, & Amanuel Melles, Selam Peacebuilding Network. "The Role of the Eritrean Diaspora in Peacebuilding and Development: Challenges and Opportunities. Toronto, Ontario: October 2006.

The Constitution Project. "Recommendations for Reforming Our Immigration Detention System and Promoting Access to Counsel in Immigration Proceedings." Washington, DC: 2009.

"The Forgetful Mr. Smith." *New York Times*. 12 July 2011.

"The Magic of Diasporas. Leader." *The Economist*. 19 November 2011, p. 13

"The Widening Dragnet." *New York Times*. 14 August 2011.

Thiollet, Helen. "*Refugees and Migrants from Eritrea to the Arab world: The cases of Sudan, Yemen and Saudi Arabia 1991-2007*." Paper prepared for the Migration and Refugee movements in the Middle East and North Africa, American University in Cairo, Egypt, 2007.

Thurian, Max & Geoffrey Wainwright. *Baptism and Eucharist: Ecumenical Convergence in Celebration*. Geneva: World Council of Churches Publications in collaboration with Grand Rapids, MI: Wm. B. Eerdmans Publishing Co., 1986.

Toledano, R Ehud. *As If Silent and Absent: Bonds of Enslavement in the Islamic Middle East*. New Haven & London: Yale University Press, 2007.

Torstrick, Rebecca and Elizabeth Faier. *Culture and Customs of the Gulf States*. Green Wood Press. West port, Connecticut, USA, 2009.

Treiber, Magnus. "*Trapped in Adolescense: The Postwar Urban Generation*" in David O'Kane & Tricia Redeker Hepner, eds. Biopolitics, Militarism, and Development: Eritrea in the Twenty-First Century. New York & Oxford, UK: Berghahn Books, (2011):92-114.

Tzouliadis, Tim. *The Forsaken: An American Tragedy in Stalin's Russia*. New York: The Penguin Press, 2008.

UN, Human Right Council, "Report of the commission of inquiry on human rights in Eritrea" 4 June 2015.

UNHCR 2014 Report: "Eritrean Refuges and asylum seekers in Europe, Ethiopia and Sudan." http://www.unhcr.org/5465fea1381.html

UNHCR: "Asylum Trends in 2013 in Europe." http://www.unhcr.org/5329b15a9.html

United Nations Council on Human Rights. "Eritrea: Submission to Universal Periodic Review," 27 June 2013. Published by Human Rights Watch. http://www.hrw.org/news/2013/06/20/eritrea-submission-universal-periodic-review.

United Nations High Commission on Refugees, "UNHCR Eligibility Guidelines for Assessing the International Protection Needs of Asylum-Seekers from Eritrea," April 2009. http://www.unhcr.org/refworld/docid/49de06122.html

United Nations Office on Drug and Crime (UNODC). "Global Reports on Trafficking in Persons." Vienna, Austria, 2014

United Nations: "International Migration Report 2013."

United States Commission on International Religious Freedom. "2010 Annual Report." May 2010.http://www.uscirf.gov/images/annual%20report%202010.pdf

United States Commission on International Religious Freedom. "2010 Annual Report," subsection on Eritrea. May 2010.

United States Commission on International Religious Freedom. "2009 Annual Report," May 2009. http://www.uscirf.gov/images/final%20ar2009%20with%20cover.pdf

United States Commission on International Religious Freedom. "2009 Annual Report, subsection on Eritrea." May 2009.

United States Department of Justice. "EOIR Immigration Court Listing." 27 November 2011.

United States Department of Justice. "Immigration Court Practice Manual." Accessed 27 November 2011.

US Department of State, Bureau of Democracy, Human Rights, and Labor, "2009 Human Rights Report," 11 March 2010.

US Department of State, Bureau of Democracy, Human Rights, and Labor. "2009 Human Rights Report: Eritrea," 11 March 2010. http://www.state.gov/g/drl/rls/hrrpt/2009/af/135952.htm

US Department of State, Bureau of Democracy, Human Rights, and Labor. "International Religious Freedom Report 2009," 26 October 2009.

US Department of State, Bureau of Democracy, Human Rights, and Labor. "International Religious Freedom Report 2009," subsection on Eritrea, 26 October 2009.

US Department of State, Office to Monitor and Combat Trafficking in Persons. "Trafficking in Persons Report: June 2011." 27 June 2011.

Visscher, Jochen, ed., & Stefan Boness, contributor. Asmara: *The Frozen City*. Berlin: Jovis; Mul ed., 2007.

Weaving the world together. Briefing: Migration and business. *The Economist*. 19 November 2011, p. 72-74: http://www.moibrahimfoundation.org/en

Whitten, Normane E. "Toward Critical Anthropology." *Journal of the American Ethnological Society*, 1988. DOI: 10.1525/ae.1988.15.4.02a00080

Wiegand, Jr, Andrew. "Eritrean Christians and the Eritrean Constitution." Global Christian.org. 2 September 2009.

WikiLeaks cables: "Eritrean Poverty and Patriotism under unhinged dictator." *The guardian.* 8 December 2010.

WikiLeaks cables: Saudi princes throw parties boasting drink, drugs and sex. 7 December 2010.http://www.theguardian.com/world/2010/dec/07/wikileaks-cables-saudi-princes-parties

Woldu, Dawit and Irv Bromall. "Africana Ethnography: How Homeland Eritrea Monitors Its American Diaspora. *Journal of Africana Studies*. Vol.7 2016.

Wrong, Michela. *I Didn't Do It for You: How the World Betrayed a Small African Nation*. New York: HarperCollins, 2005.

Zewde, Bahru ed. "Documenting the Ethiopian Student Movement: An Exercise in Oral History." Addis Ababa, Ethiopia: *Forum for Social Studies*, 2010.

ABOUT THE CONTRIBUTORS

Dawit O. Woldu is an assistant professor of Anthropology and cross-cultural Studies at the University of Houston Clear Lake who teaches courses on Social medicine, community health, and topics on African Studies. He received his Ph.D. from the University of Florida (Gainesville) in medical anthropology in 2012. A native of Eritrea, he has done extensive research on the cultural, biological, and ecological dimension of malaria and HIV/AIDS in Kenya. Dr. Woldu has also done research on Eritrean refugees and immigrants in the United States. Before, moving to the University of Houston - Clear Lake, Dr. Woldu did his postdoctoral work at Ohio University, African Studies Program, working on HIV/AIDS and substance abuse project and teaching a course on Health Research in Africa. Dr. Woldu also assisted teaching a global health course with the Global Health Initiative at Ohio University.

Irvin H. Bromall received his Ph.D. from the University of Wisconsin-Madison in 1967. He was a senior federal manager in transit-related civil rights and former political science Professor at several higher education institutions in the United States. Dr. Bromall also worked as a consultant on community development and civil society for dozens of NGO's both in the United States and other countries. After years of voluntary service to hundreds of asylum seekers and immigrants mostly from Eritrea, Ethiopia, and Mexico, Dr. Bromall passed away on March 23, 2014 at his home in Moab, UT, where he was living since he retired from the federal government two decades ago. Dr. Bromall was a very dedicated civil right advocate, who dedicated his entire life to promote social and economic justice for all.

INDEX

C

D

E

F

G

H

I

J

K

L

M

N

O

P

Q

R

S

T

U

W

Y